The Spiritual Roots of the Ecological Crisis

The Spiritual Roots of the Ecological Crisis

Jean-Claude Larchet

Translated from the French by Archibald Andrew Torrance

HOLY TRINITY PUBLICATIONS
The Printshop of St Job of Pochaev
Holy Trinity Monastery
Jordanville, New York
2022

Printed with the blessing of His Eminence,
Metropolitan Hilarion First Hierarch
of the Russian Orthodox Church Outside of Russia

Originally published *as Les Fondements spirituels de la crise écologique*
Paris: Éditions des Syrtes, 2018.

PRINTSHOP OF
SAINT JOB OF POCHAEV

An imprint of

HOLY TRINITY PUBLICATIONS
Holy Trinity Monastery
Jordanville, New York 13361-0036
www.holytrinitypublications.com

ISBN: 978-0-88465-481-0 (paperback)
ISBN: 978-0-88465-486-5 (ePub)

Library of Congress Control Number 2021952108

Cover: Underlying digital image: *Plastic bg in iceberg floating in the ocean and global warming concept* by Stokkete. Source: stock.adobe.com, 257457008.

Printed in the United States of America.

Contents

Introduction

Ecology is a recent movement which seeks to protect nature. It reacts against the manifold ways modern industrial society damages the natural environment.

Considering nature as God's creation, the various Christian confessions value it highly, and join in the movement to protect it. They make themselves heard and have come to be seen as moral authorities. The Orthodox Churches have been at the fore in this respect. The two most recent Patriarchs of Constantinople, Dimitrios I and especially Bartholomew, have been especially active. Dimitrios was the pioneer, fixing in 1988 September 1 as an annual liturgical feast dedicated to the preservation of the environment. Bartholomew has spoken and written widely on this subject. He has organized several international meetings and traveled the World to spread the Orthodox Church's message that the Creation should be protected. This strong commitment of Patriarch Bartholomew has earned him the title of the green Patriarch. The Russian Church has produced several documents on the theme of ecology and in 2015 resolved that the first Sunday in September should be a day of prayer for the protection of the environment. The Churches of Serbia, Romania, and Greece have also made several official statements in this vein.

In many Orthodox countries, rural monasteries set an example by the way they raise crops and tend flocks. They organize meetings and conferences to disseminate their work, like missionaries. In France the women's monastery of Solan is well known in this respect thanks to the many reports and articles in the national media on its work. Mount Athos is a sanctuary, free from all kinds of industrial and agricultural pollution. It is also at every level of altitude (0–2000m) a living refuge for animals and plants, like Noah's ark in the midst of a drowning world.[1]

The realization that our environment is threatened, and the ecological reaction to this, is very recent, dating from the 1970s. This reaction has an ethical character, both moral and as a way of life. It has personally inspired lovers of nature, some of whom have become famous through their competence and their struggle, which expressed through the media, has given them a certain authority. It has also led to a political movement which has gained parliamentary representation, sometimes very strong, as in Germany.

It has also acquired a spiritual dimension known as "ecospirituality." This is, mainly in the USA, strongly linked to the New Age movement and sometimes to a kind of neopaganism,[2] set up as a new religion. On this last point, Michael Crichton writes:

> If you look carefully at belief, you will see that environmentalism is, in fact, a perfect re-modelling, in the XX century, of traditional belief and of Judeo-Christian myths. There is the original Eden, a paradise, a state of grace in union with nature. There is a fall from grace into a state of pollution through eating the tree of knowledge, and finally, when all is done, a day of judgement to come for us all. We are all sinners as regards energy, all condemned to die unless we seek salvation which is now called sustainability. Sustainability is salvation in this "Church" of the environment. Organic food is its eucharistic communion, food free from pesticides which are all that good and right believing persons will touch.[3]

The Orthodox Church also sets ecology in a spiritual context, but based on a cosmology and spiritual practice developed over the centuries which give it rights of seniority. The Orthodox Church is ancient and strives to keep close to the origins of Christianity through its faithfulness to Tradition. Thus it refers constantly not simply to the Gospel but also to the teaching and experience of the Church Fathers.

At first sight one might therefore ask if the Orthodox Church, its representatives and its members are qualified to answer modern questions which were not of direct concern to those whom it takes as its reference. This applies not just to questions of bioethics arising from modern medical and biological techniques, but also to ecological problems, linked to industrialization and modern intensive agriculture.

However, it is becoming clear to more and more people that though ecological problems may need urgent political and economic solutions from governments, it is only with a radical change of mindsets and styles of living that a deep and lasting solution can be found. For ecological problems arise from spiritual roots which relate to the way man sees and relates to nature, and how he uses it. So, their solution must have a spiritual dimension.[4]

This is where the Orthodox Church can bring to the present crisis the principles which should guide the thought and action of all those who seek to save nature. They are drawn from a long tradition of thought, theological, cosmological, and anthropological on the value of the creation and how mankind should relate to it, reinforced by her liturgical and spiritual practice.

The thoughts I set forth here are a continuation of two themes which run through the greater part of my writings:

- First, different kinds of illness and their treatment. For ecology is surely a study of the illnesses of nature and how they can be treated and cured. These illnesses have their root in the spiritual sickness of mankind and their cure depends on treating this underlying sickness of mankind.
- Secondly, there is the thought of St Maximos the Confessor. He, of all the Church Fathers, is the one who went most deeply into the question of God's presence in nature and the deep relationships between all created beings and their Creator. He considers how man can relate to creatures, and through them, to God; and of the role of mediator which man is called to exercise within creation.

The synthesis of these two themes allows ecology to be approached with the correct spiritual dimension. This allows it to be treated in depth theoretically through theology, cosmology, and anthropology, and practically through ethics and asceticism. Etymologically, ethics signifies the right way of living, and asceticism, in its broadest sense, the struggle against destructive passions, and in a narrower sense, the feat of self-restraint, and wise sobriety.

Chapter 1

How It Was in the Beginning: Man's Original Relationship with Nature

THE BIBLICAL ROOTS

The Bible and the writings of the Fathers reveal that in the beginning, mankind and nature were in Paradise and this determined their relationship. This is the foundation of Orthodox thought on ecology. The Greek word, *arche*, the first word in the book of Genesis, signifies both "beginning" and "principal" or "foundation."[1] So the book of Genesis is not so much a literal historical account, as a tale rich in symbols which recounts the spiritual roots of our origins and the ends to which man and nature are called. Through this, the nature of the fall, caused by the sin of our first ancestors, is explained. Its development up to our own time is exposed, and what is made possible by Christ is revealed, the final restoration which the Church strives to fulfill.

AN ENTIRELY GOOD CREATION

The roots of Christian thought insist that the world was created by God completely good. This is repeatedly affirmed in the first chapter of Genesis which evokes the various stages of creation: "and God saw that it was good" (Gen 1:10, 12, 18, 21, 25, 31).

This goodness implies the absence of all evil and great peace and harmony amongst all creatures.[2]

MAN'S PRIVILEGED PLACE IN CREATION

Some Criticisms of Christianity

Some thinkers have sought to blame Christianity as responsible for the present ecological crisis since it affirms the superiority and power of man over nature. It is thus seen as creating a hierarchy which diminishes nature and justifies man's dominion over her and the exploitation this allows.[3] Others from the same school of thought have denounced the anthropocentric positions of Christianity in general and believe that the current crisis can only be solved by placing nature at the center and considering mankind to be just one of its elements.[4]

However, these attacks are based on assumptions foreign to the principles of Christianity, and on several misunderstandings of its true position. Several of these criticisms come from thinkers with obvious sympathies for paganism, in its Graeco-roman form, or as manifested in Nordic mythologies and shamanism. Others prefer the religions of the Far East and the New Age movement which has embraced them.

For the first group, in nature and all the beings it contains dwell gods and demi-gods or spirits. This greatly diminishes man's place as a being possessing a spirit which can bring him close to God. For the second group, the world is inhabited by gods. There are over 800 proposed by Hinduism. Often, they take the form of animals, for example Ganesh, the elephant, and Hanuman, the monkey. Every animal may be a reincarnation of a human being. All, not simply the cow, have a sacred character which puts them on the same level as man, and places man at their level. All is divine and dissolves into the great Whole, called Om in Hinduism. In the spiritually awakened, this supposedly allows the perception not just of unity and oneness, but of a total lack of differentiation. One of the principles of Hinduism, into which man is called to be initiated, is *Ta Tvam Asi*,[5] "Thou also art Om."

Buddhism is also based on the idea that all beings are to be identified with a single reality which is Nothingness, whence comes the signal importance of Emptiness to Buddhist spirituality. Man, in this vision of a world where all beings are equal, loses his superiority and singularity, and any special value. It is because of this, and the theory of reincarnation which they profess, that the religions of the Far East are impersonal in both anthropological and theological terms. Christianity bases its anthropology on the Bible, which affirms the creation in the image of God of mankind alone, called to perfect this image as resemblance. This confers the sharpest perception of the uniqueness and value of the human person and in no way accords with the anthropology of the Far East.

These critics misunderstand Christian concepts in several ways, so their meaning and outline will now be set forth.

Nature Was Created with Man in Mind, and for the Sake of Man

In the first place, there is no doubt in the Christian view that man was created by God as the crown of His creation (cf. Gen. 1:26). Moreover, the Fathers all affirm simply that all nature was created with man in mind and for his sake.[6]

St John of Damascus explains that every animal and plant has its use for man. Moreover, God ordained their use not just for man in Paradise, but also in man's fallen state which He foresaw and foreknew.[7] Of course, this usefulness is not to be seen as simply material, instrumental, and utilitarian. Nature helps man by revealing to him the beauty, wisdom, and omnipotence of God, and allows him, as we shall see later, to praise God and to rise toward Him in contemplation. St Joseph the Hesychast expresses these two qualities so simply: "All was created so that man might be nourished and admire." For example, the Sun was created not simply to heat the Earth but to embellish and adorn the World.[8]

Man, the Crown of Creation

Man is the crown of creation. When he is created, he enters a dwelling already prepared for him. He is also the most finished of all creatures for the following reasons.

1) He comes as the culmination of a line of creatures each more perfect than those which preceded it (minerals, plants, animals, etc.)
2) He recapitulates all these creatures since in him are synthesized the mineral, vegetable, and animal worlds. As the Fathers say, he is a microcosmos in a macrocosmos[9] thus including, in a certain way, all creation in himself.[10] "Man is a little world," writes St Gregory of Nyssa, "Who bears within himself all the realities of the great world."[11]

   This great world is not just the material and perceptible world, but the intelligible and immaterial world as well.[12] Man's superiority over the perceptible world arises because he is also an intelligible creature. He is superior to the intelligible world since he is also a perceptible and material being. This fact is emphasized by the Fathers when they write that because Christ assumed as man both soul and body, man becomes higher than the angels. St Gregory of Nazianzus underlines the greatness of man which comes from his twofold nature, perceptible and intelligible. This makes him a "second world," recapitulating them both as their mediator:

> Up till then, the spirit and the perceptible, distinct one from the other, remained within their own limits and bore within themselves the majesty of the Word, Creator of the world. They silently praised the greatness of the work and were its heralds everywhere. As yet there was no fusion of them, no mixture of opposites. For these are the special signs of still greater wisdom and divine magnificence before created beings. All the riches and goodness of God had not yet been revealed. So, wishing to show this forth, the Creating Word arranged that both be combined, that is both visible and invisible nature, in a living being: man. He fashions man's body from what He has already created, and from Himself he takes life which he breaths into man, a spiritual soul and an image of God as the Bible recounts. This man, a second world, great in his lowliness, He then places on the Earth as another angel, a worshipper formed from divers elements, who contemplates visible creation and is an initiate of invisible creation. He is king over the Earth and subject to what is on high, a being both earthly and heavenly, ephemeral and immortal, visible and intelligible, a mediator between greatness and lowliness, both spirit and flesh.[13]

3) Though a plant just has the soul of a plant and an animal, the soul of an animal, man possesses, over and above his rational and intellective soul, a will, the capacity for self-determination which allows him to be free.[14]
4) Man was created and modeled in the image and likeness of God (Gen 1:26–27), which is not the case for any other being in nature. Man is in the image of God especially through his intellect, his reason, and his will,[15] his capacity for self-determination. He is in the likeness of God through the various virtues which dwell in him,[16] at first just as seeds which he is personally called to cultivate.

5) For this reason, man is not just a microcosm, but so to say, a *microtheos*, a little god[17] as St Gregory of Nyssa asserts. For were man to be but a microcosm, he could be seen as a synthesis of earthly elements which are also to be found in "mice and mosquitos,"[18] and he could be seen as swallowed up by the material universe instead of embracing it.[19] Thus, as says St Gregory of Nazianzus, he is also another universe within the Universe, great in his lowliness.[20]
6) Man is crowned by God as "the king of creation,"[21] and it is precisely for this reason that he is created last of all creatures as St Gregory of Nyssa explains:

> It would not have been natural for the overlord to make his entrance ahead of his subjects. It was only after his kingdom had been made ready that the king could reasonably be revealed, when the Creator of the Universe had, so to say, made ready the throne of him who was to reign. Behold the earth, the isles, the sea, and above them the vault of heaven like a roof. All manner of riches was placed within this palace. By riches, I mean the whole creation, all that the earth germinates and brings forth, the whole perceptible world, lively and living. Also amongst these riches should be numbered all those things whose beauty makes them precious in the sight of man, gold, silver and precious stones, so greatly desired: all those treasures which God hides abundantly in the depths of the earth as in a royal storehouse [...].
>
> This is why man is brought in last to the creation. It is not that he is despised and placed at the lowest level, but because, from his birth, he was destined to be king over his domain. A good householder does not invite in a guest before making ready the meal; but when everything is tidy as it should be, and the table, bedchamber and house well adorned, with dinner ready he invites in his guest. In the same way, He Who in His great riches is the host of our nature, first decorates the dwelling with all kinds of beauty and prepares a great feast of varied dishes. Then he brings in man, not to bestow on him the goods which he has not yet acquired, but the enjoyment of what he is offered. This is why, in creating him, he lays a double foundation by mixing the divine and the earthly, so that through the quality of each, man should naturally enjoy both God through his divine nature, and earthly goods through his feelings which are of the same kind as these goods.[22]

God then grants man dominion over all creatures. The book of Genesis makes this clear: "Let us make man in Our image, according to Our likeness. Let them have dominion over the fish of the sea, over the birds of heaven, over the cattle, and over all the earth, and over every creeping thing that moves upon the earth" (Gen 1:26); "Then God blessed them, and God said unto them, 'Be fruitful and multiply; fill the earth, and subdue it, and have dominion over the fish of the sea, over the birds of heaven, and over every living thing that moves on the earth'" (Gen 1:28). After the flood, these last words are repeated

> Thus God blessed Noah and his sons, and said unto them, "Increase fruitful, and multiply, and fill the earth, and have dominion over it. For the dread and fear of you shall be upon all the wild animals of the earth, all the birds of heaven, all that move upon the earth, and all the fish of the sea. I have put them under your authority."
>
> (Gen 9:1–2)

These three passages emphasize dominion over the animals, but the phrase "and multiply, and fill the earth, and have dominion over it" has universal import. It applies also to the vegetable and mineral world. Other passages indicate that God gives plants for man's use, to fulfil his needs: "Then God said, 'Behold, I have given you every seed-bearing herb that sows seed on the face of all the earth, and every tree whose fruit yields seed; to you it shall be for food'" (Gen 1:29). This also indicates man's mastery of nature, but has less need of emphasis than his dominion over animals which can move, and so more easily escape him.

The power over animals which God gives to man seems to embarrass certain contemporary authors since they wish to make man just one of nature's parts; but the Fathers accept it with ease.[23] They consider that this power flows naturally from the fact that man is in the image and likeness of Him who orders everything,[24] and also from his intellect[25] and power of self-determination which the animals lack.[26] They also affirm that man needs this power to accomplish the mission given to him in God's creation, which is not just material but mainly and especially spiritual.[27]

7) Man, in his essence is a part of nature, a creature and a microcosm, and also the image and likeness of God. His vocation is to unite within himself

the extremes of the created world and to bring all creatures to God in contemplation and thanksgiving, imparting to the created world for its benefit the grace he has received from God. Man is privileged to be placed at the center as mediator between God and creation. When the Word of God takes flesh to accomplish His saving work, He is explicitly called the Mediator. For in fact He comes to take up, restore, and complete the task of the first man who, through sin, lamentably failed to fulfill it.[28]

The commandment given by God to the first of mankind: "Be fruitful and multiply" (Gen 1:28) has been specially condemned by the modern thinkers quoted above as being the most explicit Judeo-Christian source of the tendency of man to exploit nature, and even of the ideology of endless progress so common in modern civilization, yet already present in past times. But in this way, they twice contradict themselves. Taken at face value, this commandment was given to encourage the development of the human race, which at that time consisted of just two persons. The same words were also spoken to all living creatures (Gen 1:22).[29] At a deeper level, many Fathers teach that it should also be understood anagogically as referring to the spiritual growth of man and his increase in virtue.[30]

It is also possible to see here a command to cultivate plants and pasture animals, but it is quite out of the question that the aim of this should be consumption or commercial gain. Commerce came much later in the history of human beings, who at first used barter to exchange their goods. The eating of meat was forbidden in the beginning since it meant taking the life of animals and spilling their blood. The first men lived by gathering the fruits of plants which grew naturally in the wild. For thousands of years this was the way of life, and even in our day it satisfies the needs of "primitive" or "archaic" people as ethnologists can testify. It is true that the command to cultivate the earth is given in Genesis (cf. Gen 2:5), and St Theophilos of Antioch remarks that "God placed man in Paradise so that he should work."[31] But before his sin, this work was painless for man (cf. Gen 3:17–18), and several purposes may be seen in this:

- To keep in man's mind that God is his master;[32]
- To remind him "that he may only enjoy this garden of delights if he takes care of it;"[33]

- To involve man in the process of creation and preservation of the life which God had ordained, for, as the Orthodox Tradition makes plain, man's spiritual life is always a synergy, or collaboration, between his own effort and grace. The book of Genesis sees cultivation as part of this second purpose: "Then the Lord God took the man He formed and put him in the garden to tend and keep it" (Gen 2:15).

THE CREATION: AN EXPRESSION OF THE LOVE, GREATNESS, WISDOM, AND BEAUTY OF THE CREATOR

Nature in all its aspects was created for man, the highest creature, who is called to have dominion over it and to take up the central task of mediation. But despite all this, and despite the fact that the Fathers emphasize how this means that the world was made for man,[34] it is wrong to have a wholly anthropocentric view of creation, seeing it solely in relation to man.

Creation took place through an overflowing of the Love of God. By an act of Will and not by a natural emanation He brought all beings, other than Himself, into existence. To them He gives His Love; and they, according to their several abilities, can relate to Him by returning His Love. St John of Damascus has this to say:

> As God is good, and beyond all goodness, He was not content to contemplate Himself alone; but through His overflowing goodness it pleased Him to bring forth beings who would profit from His liberality and participate in His goodness. He brings from non-being to being and creates the whole universe, visible and invisible, and man, composed of both the visible and invisible.[35]

God creates all creatures in love, not just the angels and man, even if He does love man most of all, as is shown most clearly by the divine Word becoming man to save and deify him.

The creatures themselves bear witness to the love of God which created them; and by their profusion, their diversity, their energy and magnificence, as well as by the order which governs each species, they show forth His omnipotence, His greatness, His wisdom, and His beauty.[36] The saints who see the depths of things through the purity of their spirit perceive the relationships which unite naturally the creatures to God. And even if there were no man to see this, the angels would. Moreover, in the depths of the forest of the Amazon basin there are multitudes of wondrous plants and animals which no man has ever seen; and in the heavens a multitude of constellations and stars which no human eye has detected and which, perhaps, no man may ever see.

The Holy Scripture bears witness to the glorification of God by His creatures, each in its own way: "Day unto day uttereth speech, and night unto night sheweth knowledge. There is neither speech nor language, in which their voices are not heard. Their sound is gone out into all the earth, and their words unto the ends of the world" (Ps 18:3–4 LXX).

Dostoyevsky writes: "Each blade of grass, each insect, an ant, a gilded bee, [...] witness to the divine mystery and fulfil it themselves continually."[37] St Nicholas (Velimirovich) recalls that when Christ died, all the orders of the creatures were troubled:

> Every dumb and inanimate creature trembled and protested in its own way with its own language. The dumb earth shook—this is its language. The rocks were rent—this is their language. The Sun hid its light—this is its language. All inanimate creatures protested in their own ways. For all these inanimate creatures are subject to Him as once in Paradise they were subject to Adam. For all the inanimate creatures know Him as once they knew Adam in Paradise. How it could be possible that creatures without senses should know Him and obey Him, we cannot tell. This comes from the inner sensitivity of these creatures imparted by the word with which God created them. [...] The earth shook, the rocks were rent, and the Sun hid its rays as much in anger as in pain. All nature was afflicted by the sufferings of the One who had called them from non-being and bid them rejoice in their being. It was as if they said: "With whom will I be left and who will sustain me now, when He who upholds all things suffers death?"[38]

He then invites all created beings to celebrate the Saviour's resurrection in a poem which has become a much-loved song in Serbia:

Peoples exult, nations give ear:
Christ is arisen bringing us joy!
Dance ye stars, ye mountains sing:
Christ is arisen bringing us joy!
Whisper ye forests blow ye winds:
Christ is arisen bringing us joy!
Thunder ye seas and roar ye beasts:
Christ is arisen bringing us joy!
Hum ye bees and sing ye birds:
Christ is arisen bringing us joy!
Let the heavens bow down and the earth arise:
Christ is arisen bringing us joy!

ALL CREATURES ARE LINKED TO THE DIVINE WORD IN THEIR ORIGIN AND THEIR END

All creatures are linked, above all, to the Divine Word. They were conceived within Him even before their creation. He it was who fixed the moment of their appearing and in Him they subsist and have their ending. The Church Fathers have fully developed all these aspects, but they can already be found in several passages from the New Testament. The Gospel according to St John begins thus: "In the beginning was the Word, and the Word was with God, and the Word was God. He was in the beginning with God. All things were made through Him, and without Him nothing was made that was made" (John 1:1–3). The epistle to the Colossians states that all things were created not just in Him and by Him but for Him: "For by Him all things were created that are in heaven and that are on earth, visible and invisible, whether thrones or dominions or principalities or powers. All things were created through Him and for Him. And He is before all things, and in Him all things consist" (Col 1:16–17).

St Maximos the Confessor develops these affirmations theologically in his theory of the *logoi* to which we will return.

THE ETHICAL AND SPIRITUAL LIMITS OF MAN'S POWER OVER CREATION

God did not grant unlimited power over creation to mankind. In principle, man may make use of all creatures, but only to fulfil his true needs—what is really necessary.[39] God gives man plants for nourishment, but does not by this make him a consumer or an exploiter. Man receives plants as a gift for food, but not for unlimited use (cf. Gen. 1:29–30).

Man's God-given power over animals is in no way out of the ordinary. What would be strange would be domination of man by animals, something which only creators of science fiction in books or films can imagine. But nowhere is it said that God gave man the power to exploit the animals or to use them for trade or even to eat them. The biblical text states that both man and animals receive vegetables and fruits for food (Gen. 1:29–30), but there is no idea that animals may be eaten. A vegetarian diet is the norm in paradise[40] and likewise it also becomes the norm for Orthodox monks who strive to regain paradise. It is also followed by all during the periods of fasting which take up more than half the year in the Orthodox Church and is thus, as St Basil says, "A faithful image of[41] the earthly paradise."

The power given to man over the animals is mainly a power of organization as St Basil the Great suggests,[42] and as illustrated by certain frescos of paradise. Some translations use "dominate," but others "have dominion over," which suggests a more spiritual power. This interpretation is confirmed by another passage from Genesis: "Also, God formed out of the ground all the wild animals of the field and all the birds of heaven, and brought them to Adam to see what he would call them. Thus whatever Adam called each living creature, that was its name. So Adam gave names to all the cattle, to all the birds of heaven, and to all the wild animals of the field" (Gen 2:19–20).

This power of naming creatures indicates a certain spiritual knowledge of creatures, of their properties and the laws which govern their nature.[43] It also shows man's spiritual power over them.[44] In the thought of traditional societies, there is a natural link between names and what they designate. This receives philosophical justification from Plato in his *Cratylus*: to know the name of something is, in a certain way, to appropriate it and master it spiritually. St Maximos the Confessor goes further into this spiritual insight. For him, the names given to the creatures correspond to their *logoi*, their spiritual essence in relation to God. He is the principle of the *logoi* and their culmination. They are the good will of God, or His divine plan which in them is expressed. We will return to this point.

Other Fathers give even less importance to the physical and material meaning of the biblical texts which give power to man over the animals. They bring out their anagogical meaning, seeing them as an expression of man's inner power over his own animal nature. For instance, St Ambrose of Milan writes:

> The beasts of the field and the birds of the air represent our irrational impulses. There are both small and great beasts just as there are different bodily passions, some violent and others enervating. As for the birds of the air, they are simply vain thoughts, which like birds, flutter around our soul and draw it away, hither and thither.[45]

In the works of Origen and St Basil, ssimilar ideas can be found.[46]

Looking at the material meaning of these biblical texts, it can be seen that even though God gives man dominion over the plants and animals, He Himself remains their master: they are His. Thus in Deuteronomy we read: "Indeed, heaven and heaven of heaven belong to the Lord your God, also, the earth and everything in it" (Deut 10:14), and in Psalm 23/24: "The earth is the Lord's, and the fullness thereof" (Ps 23:1 LXX) or in Job: "That in His hand is the life of every living thing" (Job 12:10).

We can see the confirmation of this in man's calling to make use of the produce of nature in an eucharistic offering of them back to God with thanksgiving for the gifts He has given us. As the Orthodox Liturgy has it: "Thine Own of Thine Own, we offer unto Thee, in behalf of all and for all."[47]

At all events, man's use of creatures should be reasonable and good. This is shown by the commandment given to Adam and Eve not to eat of the tree of knowledge of good and evil. This sets an ethical and spiritual limit to how man may deal with creatures. According to St Maximos the Confessor, this divine command forbids man to enjoy creatures through their physical appearances and instead helps him to remain related to them through contemplation. Once man had transgressed this commandment, his perception and use of creatures changed radically, so that he sought in them the means to satisfy his passions, rooted in sin.

MAN: GUEST AND STEWARD OF CREATION

The world is not given to man as a mine of resources to be exploited, but rather as a house[48] of which he is the tenant, and which he should maintain, as French leases state: "like a good head of his household." The rent to be paid to God is thanksgiving for all he has received.

All that has been stated above also shows that man should not be seen so much as a master, but as the servant of the Master. Many biblical texts, some cited above, remind us that God is the only King, Lord and Master, and that man can be no more than an image of the King and Lord, or the servant of the Master: a steward of the Master's goods.

This view of man as a steward, expressed by certain Fathers, needs some explanation. Clearly, he is not called upon to manage an estate for an economic profit. He is not to farm nature as a commercial enterprise. He is called to use nature wisely and to help maintain its life and stability.

MAN: THE KEEPER OF CREATION

God also set man to be the keeper of creation (Gen 2:15),[49] to protect it and keep it safe. When God permitted man to eat of all the fruits except for the fruit of the tree of the knowledge of good and evil (Gen 2:16–17), it was to keep him from evil and suffering its effects; but it was also to prevent evil infecting the creation which would then bear the consequences.

THE SPIRITUAL USE OF CREATION

So far, we have dealt with man's relationship to creation in mainly physical and material terms: man's power over creatures and his consumption of them. This is necessary today in view of the secular nature of the current ecological debate, which rarely takes account of any spiritual dimension. However, it is obvious that creation is far greater than the use man can make of it, and amongst the vast multitude of creatures only a small minority can be of any use. So it is clear that the relationship of man with creation must be set against a much wider background than what is usually proposed.

We have already given a few brief examples of the anagogical and spiritual interpretations which the Fathers commonly give of the book of Genesis. It is important to remember this point, which insists that the relationship between man and creatures in the beginning was defined as being ideally contemplative and eucharistic. So it is within these two kinds of relationship that man is called to his God-given function of mediator.

THE PRESENCE OF GOD IN CREATION

Before explaining what all this means, it must be said that Christianity considers creation to have been sanctified from the beginning by being the work of God and bearing His imprint. These are clearly grounds of the greatest importance for respecting nature. As Dostoyevsky wrote in *The Brothers Karamazov*, "If God does not exist then everything is permitted." Clearly, only God can provide an absolute foundation for morals and ethics in any domain, since only He is absolute. Unmoored from God, all morals become relative and a cause for argument.

The imprint of God on creation takes several forms.

God, Everywhere Present in Creation

God, Who created the world and continues through His providence to preserve it, is present everywhere. The Fathers have a keen perception of this constant and universal presence.[50] A basic prayer of the Orthodox Church, recited several times a day by the faithful, calls upon the Holy Spirit as "everywhere present and filling all things." St Gregory of Nyssa expresses this omnipresence of God very strongly:

> Who, when beholding the Universe, is so faint-hearted as not to believe that the Godhead is in everything, that The Godhead is clothed with the Universe, embraces it and dwells there? For what exists depends on Him Who is, and nothing which exists can do so but in Him Who is. All things are in Him and He is in all things.[51]

This consciousness of God's omnipresence is still lively in contemporary Orthodox spiritual figures like St Joseph the Hesychast who bear witness to their experience of this reality:

> God is everywhere. There is no place where He cannot be found. Within and without, above and below, wherever you turn all things cry out: "God." We live and move in Him (cf. Acts 17:28). We breath God, we eat God, we clothe ourselves in God. All things praise and bless God. The whole creation cries out. All things, living or inanimate, speak with wonder and glorify the Creator. "Let everything that hath breath praise the Lord!" (Ps 150:5).[52]

The Divine Energies

The foremost way in which God manifests His presence in nature is through His divine energies which infuse all creatures with divine qualities. St Paul brings this out in the Epistle to the Romans, saying: "For since the creation of the world His invisible attributes are clearly seen, being understood by the things that are made, even His eternal power and Godhead" (Rom 1:20). St Maximos the Confessor puts it this way:

> We know God, not in His essence, but through the magnificence of His creation and the action of His providence which show us, as in a mirror, the reflection of His goodness, His wisdom and His infinite power.[53]

In the thought of the Greek Fathers, the divine energies manifest the essence by shining forth from it into the Cosmos, which leads them to describe them as "that which surrounds the essence." God manifests and communicates Himself through them whilst remaining transcendent, hidden, and incommunicable in His essence itself, beyond compare with any creature. In the same way, it is possible for creatures to participate in Him and even to be divinized in the measure that their natures are able to receive it. Yet even so, they do not acquire His essence or become divine by nature. St Gregory Palamas expresses this matter thus:

> God is, and is said to be, the nature of all creatures insofar as they all participate in Him and are constituted by this participation. They do not

> participate in His nature, far from it. It is in His energy that they participate. He is the entity embracing all beings, the form of all forms as their origin and source, the wisdom of the wise, and, in a word, all in all. Moreover, He is not a nature since He is beyond all nature. He is not a being, for He is above all beings. He is not a form, and has no form, since He surpasses all forms.[54]

The theological distinction between the essence, or nature, and the divine energies explains how God can be present and active in the world without being part of the world, without the world being God Himself (pantheism), or without the world being in Him (panentheism).[55] The uncreated character of the Divine virtues and activities is thus preserved, and the incoherent idea of created grace, invented by the scholastics in the medieval West, is avoided. The divine energies may penetrate creatures, but in no way become part of their natural character. Moreover, the Orthodox do not consider the energies as a force, or an array of forces, energies in the physical sense. Nor are they "the soul of the world," an idea found in the cosmologies of the pantheist religions of the Far East.[56]

Pagan pantheism appears to place the highest value on nature by identifying it with God himself; but it leads to the reduction of God to nature and to the idolatry of creatures. This, as St Gregory Palmas points out, flies in the face of God Himself:

> We sing praises and are filled with wonder as we contemplate the great work of God, the sum of the visible creation. The wise pagans praised it also and were filled with wonder at what they beheld. But we do this for the glory of the Creator whereas they demean it. For they in their wretchedness have "served the creature more than the Creator" (Rom 1: 25).[57]

Pantheism also demeans the creatures themselves. Since they are all identified with the same divine reality, they lose their identity and their individual value which Christian Theology preserves through the doctrines of Divine energies and the *logoi*.[58]

These energies are not simply passive attributes of God which shine out from Him into the creation. They are His activities.[59] The Greek word *energia* is often translated by "activity" or "operation" which signifies that God does not simply shine forth but also acts in His creation. The creation is not just the result of an original command, but exists through God's untiring care,[60] which has led some Western theologians to speak of "immanent and continuous creation." Christ proclaims, "My Father has been working until now, and I have been working" (John 5:17) and in the Acts of the Apostles we read: "God, who made the world and everything in it, since He is Lord of heaven and earth, [...] He gives to all life, breath, and all things. [...] He is not far from each one of us; for in Him we live and move and have our being" (Acts 17:24–28). St John Chrysostom remarks laconically: "Nothing can remain alive without the help of Providence."[61] And St Maximos the Confessor writes:

> God, Who through His energy brings all about, but remains unchanging, is the beginning, the middle and the end of all creatures [...] He is the beginning since He is the Creator; He is the middle since it is He Who provides; and He is the end since it is He Who brings to completion. Indeed, it is said that all is in Him, by Him and for Him. (Rom 11:36)[62]

God's active presence in His creation is expressed thus by St Irenaeus of Lyon:

> Who can grasp His hand which measures the immeasurable, and compasses the measure of the heavens? In it is held the earth and all its depths, which contains "the breadth, and length, and depth, and height" (Eph 3:18) of the whole creation, of that which is seen stretched out before us, and that which is incomprehensible and invisible? This is why "Far above all principality, and power, and might, and dominion, and every name that is named" (Eph 1:21), to whatever creature they belong, there is God. He it is Who fills the heavens (Jr 23:24) and "beholdest the depths" (Dan 3:55). He is also with each of us: "Am I a God at hand, saith the LORD, and not a God afar off. Can any hide himself in secret places that I shall not see him? (Jer 23:2–24). For in His hand are all things. His hand lightens the heavens and that which is beneath the heavens and "searcheth the reins and hearts" (Rev 2:23). It penetrates our secret depths and clearly nourishes and keeps us.[63]

A long description of God's action in the world can be found in the works of St Theophilos of Antioch who likens it to the work of a pilot steering a ship.

> Just as the soul, enclosed in the human body, is hidden from our sight and shows itself through the movements of the body, so God, though invisible, shows Himself clearly through His providence and His works. When you see a ship with full sails sailing over sea and steering towards the shore, you have no doubt that the steersman directs it. Can you doubt that that there is a God, master of the universe, who moves it, simply because your bodily eyes cannot see Him? [...] No one doubts the existence of a king of the earth even though most of his subjects never see him. He makes himself known through his laws and decrees, his power and his armies, and images in his likeness. So, do not the omnipotence of God and the beauty of His works make Him known?
>
> Consider, O man, the nature of His works: the periodic hardships of the seasons; the changes in the atmosphere; the admirable succession of the days, the nights the months and the years; the huge variety of seeds, of plants and fruits; the different kinds of creature which walk or creep upon the earth, which fly in the air or which swim in the waters; the instinct given to each of them to multiply and to feed their young, not for their own sakes but for the use of man; Providence which fillest all things living with plenteous food; the obedience which all are commanded to give to man; the ceaseless flow of fountains and rivers, the abundance of rain and dew to water the earth at different seasons; the various movements of the heavenly bodies; the rising of the morning star which heralds the rising of a far more brilliant star [...]; the course [...] of [...] heavenly bodies inscribed in the sky by that infinite wisdom which has given all these stars their true names. He only is God, Who caused light to shine in the darkness and brought it forth from His bosom; Who set bounds to the sea and has given the treasures of hail and snow; Who has gathered the waters into the depths of the abyss and has buried darkness in its black fastness to bring forth that tender light, so sweet and desirable for mortals; Who calls the clouds from the ends of the earth and sends forth lightning from them; Who hurls the thunderbolt to terrify the world, but warns us with the lightning flash

lest the sudden shock should cause us suddenly to fall; Who moderates the violence of the lightning which falls from heaven lest it should consume the earth; for if thunder and lightning were left unchecked they would turn all things to ashes and after their passage only ruins would remain.

He alone is my God. The Lord of all Who has stretched out the heavens and set limits to the earth; Who stirs up the depths of the oceans and arouses the roar of the waves; Who reigns over the power of the sea and calms the rolling billows; Who has set the earth upon the waters and imparted to it the means of life; in a word, Who enlivens all things by His Spirit, for if He were to withdraw it into Himself, all would return to the void. It is by this Spirit, O man, that you speak; it is by Him that you breath.[64]

The 28th Discourse of St Gregory Nazianzus[65] and the 5th Discourse on Providence of St Theodoret of Cyrus[66] contain similar long and fine accounts. They see in the admirable arrangement of creation in its different forms clear signs of the active presence of God …

A fine passage from St Nicholas (Velimirovich) shows with poetic delicacy how God, in His Providence, continually perfects the works of animals and man:

Man casts a seed into the field and leaves it to God, […] and God watches over the seed for a hundred days, protecting and warming it, quickening it and steadily causing it to grow up from the ground as a shoot. Then He fills this shoot with grain and ripens it until man returns to the field and harvests the grain in a day or two, carrying it off into his barn.

The raven lays its eggs then leaves them and takes no more care of them. But God takes upon Himself to watch carefully over the little chicks both day and night. The fish leave their eggs and depart, but God remains and takes care that these eggs become little fish which can feed and grow. Numberless orphans of both men and animals would have disappeared had God not taken care of them. Day and night, God watches over all His creatures, hearkens to their requests and satisfies their needs.[67]

THE *LOGOI*

The second kind of imprint which God imparts to creation is what St Maximos the Confessor calls *logoi.*[68] The *logos* of a being is its essential principal or reason. It is what defines it fundamentally[69] and gives it its unique character, but it is also its end, what it is called to be. It is what causes it to be, both its principal and its final end. This principal and this end are in God, which is why the word *logos* has a meaning which is spiritual rather than philosophical.[70]

A particular being corresponds to its own *logos* which defines it and makes of it a distinct and unique individual,[71] and which gives it its own value and destiny in relation to God. Thus there is a *logos* for every being which exists, which has existed or which will exist. Moreover, there is a *logos* which defines its essence or nature, a *logos* which places it in a species, a *logos* which gives it a gender and a multitude of *logoi* which give it the wealth of qualities which define its essence.[72] An individual does not simply correspond to one unique *logos,* but to a multitude of *logoi* many of which correspond also to other beings. Thus some *logoi* are particular and others universal,[73] so a recapitulation of the *logoi* is possible by passing from the particular to the universal.[74]

The *logoi* of all beings were determined together by God[75] before all ages[76] in the Divine Logos, the Word of God, that is, before these beings were created.[77] It is in Him that they were to be found from before time began and in Him that they subsist without variation.[78]

All things are known by God through their *logoi,* even before they are called into being.[79] So every being, through its *logos,* exists potentially in God from before the ages. But it is only at the moment when God, in His wisdom, decides to create it that it exists as an act through the same *logos.*[80] Once created according to this *logos,* this same *logos* is the pattern by which God, in His Providence, preserves it and makes its potential bloom.[81] However, looking at these three moments, it can be said that every being has not only a *logos* by which its essence is predefined, but also a *logos* which predefines its coming to be.[82]

The *logoi* of beings are not manifestations of the divine essence but of God's creative Will.[83] For this reason, St Maximos, following Dionysios the Areopagite, calls the *logoi* divine "wills,"[84] but more especially because they are, in all beings, the inscription of the divine Will and intention for each, and they make manifest God's plan in creation.[85]

The following passage from *Ambigua to John* describes well the presence of the *logoi* in creation and their recapitulation in the creating Word:

> Anyone considering that with reason and wisdom God brought beings from non-being to being, will little by little bring his soul to contemplate the infinite variety of beings in nature and thus to discern, through reflection and intelligent examination, the *logos* through which each was created. Will he not then see simply a multitude of *logoi* within the unique Logos, indivisibly distinguished by the differences between created beings which come from their specific individuality which remains unconfused both within them and with respect to one another? Moreover, would he not also know that this multitude of *logoi* are one, as all are raised up without confusion to Him Who is the essential and hypostatical Word of God the Father, the origin and cause of all things. "For by him were all things created, that are in heaven, and that are in earth, visible and invisible, whether they be thrones, or dominions, or principalities, or powers: all things were created by him, and for him" (Col 1, 16). Before all ages He contained within Himself the pre-existing *logoi* of created beings. When, by His good Will He formed from non-being the substance of the visible and invisible worlds He modelled them on these *logoi*. By His Word and His Wisdom He creates and created all things, universal and particular, when their time was ripe. We believe, then, that before the ages He established the *logos* of the creation of angels, the *logos* of the creation of every nature and power which fills the world from on high, the *logos* of mankind, and without naming them all, the *logos* of each being which draws its existence from God. Moreover, we believe that He is the same Who in Himself is above all, infinite, ineffable, unknowable and above every creature and above all possible difference and distinction which exist or can be conceived therein. He is the Same Who reveals Himself and multiplies Himself in all that comes forth from Him, in due measure to each according to the measure of His goodness. He recapitulates them all in Himself, from Whom comes the being and stability from which they all came to be, and for Whom they were all created, who live and move and have their being in God. Thus all of them, inasmuch as they have come forth from God, participate in their own measure in God, by their intellect, by their

> reason, by their feelings, by their vital movements or by the essential quality of being what they are, as was revealed to the great Dionysios the Areopagite, the seer of God.[86]

The following passage from *Questions to Thalassios* expresses well how the *logoi* lead man to God through their contemplation:

> Once God had established all visible nature, He did not leave it to be moved solely by the perceptible. For He sowed in each species which fills it the spiritual *logoi* both of wisdom and well-ordered ways of behavior. Thus not only was the Author of all creatures, He Who is revealed by the *logoi* of created beings, loudly proclaimed by creatures which have no speech, but also man, taught by the laws and manner of being of visible realities, can easily find the right way which leads to Him.
>
> This then, is way of the highest Goodness. It does not simply establish the divine and bodiless essences of intelligible beings as images of the ineffable divine glory. According to the divine law and in proportion to their being, they receive the incomprehensible splendor of that Beauty beyond our ken. Moreover, it mixes with perceptible realities, which are far from limited to intelligible essences, those expressions of Its own greatness which are capable of leading unerringly to God a human intellect which allows itself to be guided by them.[87]

Creatures as Symbols

St Maximos the Confessor writes that we "hear all creation proclaim with one clear voice its own Author."[88] Many texts in the Old Testament and the New, in the Liturgy and the Fathers make the world appear as a witness to the glory of God, to His Beauty, His omnipotence, and His wisdom. Psalm 18/19 puts it thus:

> The heavens declare the glory of God, and the firmament showeth His handy-work. Day unto day uttereth speech, and night unto night sheweth knowledge. There is neither speech nor language, in which their voices

are not heard. Their sound is gone out into all the earth, and their words unto the ends of the world." (Ps 18:3–4 LXX)

Psalm 103/104 evokes the wonders of creation and the relationship with God of all the beings it contains. Psalm 148 invites all creatures to praise God:

> Praise Him, sun and moon; praise Him, all ye stars and light. Praise Him, ye heaven of heavens, and thou water that art above the heavens. Let them praise the Name of the Lord; for He spake, and they came to be; He commanded, and they were created. [...] Praise the Lord from the earth, ye dragons, and all deeps; Fire and hail, snow and ice, the stormy wind, fulfilling His word; Mountains and all hills, fruitful trees and all cedars; Beasts and all cattle, creeping things and feathered fowls; [...] Let them praise the Name of the Lord, for His Name only is exalted; His praise is above heaven and earth. (Ps 148:3–13 LXX)

St Paul writes that "His invisible *attributes* are clearly seen, being understood by the things that are made, *even* His eternal power and Godhead" (Rom 1:20). St Basil remarks that "in the smallest details [of creation] can be seen the greatness of divine wisdom,"[89] and that "a plant or a blade of grass is enough to draw all our thought to contemplate the art which brought such things to be."[90]

The Fathers often draw attention to the symbolic character of creatures as they relate to God and to spiritual life. They do not see them as isolated beings, enclosed in themselves, but as witnesses, each in its own way, to a relationship to God, or to a virtue which man should follow in his spiritual life, or to a passion which he should avoid.

They see in the arrangement and brightness of the stars and in the alternance of day and night a form of the glorification of God. As the Psalmist puts it:

> The heavens declare the glory of God, and the firmament showeth His handy-work. Day unto day uttereth speech, and night unto night sheweth knowledge. There is neither speech nor language, in which their voices

> are not heard. Their sound is gone out into all the earth, and their words unto the ends of the world." (Ps 18:3–4 LXX)

There are also liturgical texts which echo the same idea. For example, there is this extract from the prayer for the blessing of the waters at Theophany:

> Great art Thou, O Lord, and marvelous are Thy works: no words suffice to sing the praise of Thy wonders. [...] The sun sings Thy praises; the moon glorifies Thee; the stars supplicate before Thee; the light obeys Thee; the deeps are afraid at Thy presence; the fountains are Thy servants. Thou hast stretched out the heavens like a curtain; Thou hast established the earth upon the waters; Thou hast walled about the sea with sand. Thou hast poured forth the air that living things may breathe.[91]

In the song of birds and in all the sounds made by animals, the Fathers see a prayer to God. They see a prayer in the beauty of the flowers which open to the Sun, and in the movement and rustling of the grass, in the whispering of the breeze in the branches, in the splashing of water and the crackling of the fire. For example, St Joseph the Hesychast, a contemporary Orthodox Saint writes:

> All creatures, living or inanimate sing hymns to God, some with their voices, others with their leaves. Each has its own special voice. Even a little blade of grass upon which you tread cries out: the perfume it diffuses is its own voice.[92]

For the Fathers, the character and behavior of each kind of animal bring lessons and sometimes models for spiritual life. Here is the advice of the book of Job:

> But now ask the four-footed animals if they may speak to you, and the birds of the air if they may report to you. Tell the earth if it may interpret it to you, the fish of the sea will explain to you. Who among all these does not know the hand of the Lord created them, that in His hand is the life of every living thing and the breath of every man? (Job 12:7–9)

Christ Himself gives the birds of the sky as examples of trust in God's Providence, for: "they neither sow nor reap nor gather into barns;" and "the lilies of the field, how they grow; they neither toil nor spin" (Matt 6: 26–28).

Long and beautiful commentaries on these subjects can be found in the letters of St Theophilos of Antioch,[93] in the homilies of St Basil,[94] of St Gregory of Nazianzus[95] and of St John Chrysostom,[96] and in the discourses on Providence of St Theodoret of Cyrus.[97]

The creation is a book full of spiritual teaching. An apothegm reveals that for St Anthony, Nature was the only book:

> One of the wise men of old came to the righteous Anthony and said to him: "How can you hold fast, O Father, when you are deprived of the consolation of books?" He replied: "My book, O philosopher, is nature and its beings, and it is always with me when I wish to read the words of God."[98]

The creation is a world of symbols, where each creature has a message about the Creator, and he who will read or listen to it is raised up to Him. St Maximos the Confessor shows that the whole perceptible world is a symbol of the intelligible, and that the spirit which is well trained can see the one in the other:

> The whole world of beings which has issued from God through creation is divided into the intelligible world, filled with bodiless and intellectual essences, and the perceptible world, bodily and magnificently woven with a wealth of forms and natures [...].
>
> For it is in its entirety that the intelligible world appears in mystical fashion in the totality of the perceptible world through symbolic figures for those who are able to see them. Likewise, the entire perceptible world becomes so simple in the intelligible world that it can be known through the intellect thanks to the *logoi*. Thus the second lies in the first through the *logoi*, and the first in the second through the figures. And as said Ezekiel, that wonderful seer of higher realities, the whole work is "like a wheel within a wheel" speaking, in my opinion, of these two worlds. Moreover, "For the invisible things of him from the creation of the

> world are clearly understood in creatures by thought," as says the divine Apostle. So, as it is written, that which does not appear becomes visible through that which does appear. And, with greater reason, that which appears can be conceived in the thought of those who apply themselves to its spiritual interpretation through that which does not appear. For the symbolic interpretation of intelligible things through visible things is the spiritual knowledge and contemplation of what is seen through the invisible. Beings, then, which manifest each other must assuredly reflect each other truly and clearly, and be related without falsehood to these reflections.[99]

CREATURES ARE DUE BOTH RESPECT AND VENERATION

Creatures are related to God through the divine energies which dwell within them and the *logoi*. They are also signs and symbols of the spiritual world which transcends them but in no way diminishes their own worth. Instead, it gives them extra worth which makes them worthy of respect, and even more of veneration and love. A contemporary Orthodox spiritual elder, St Paisios of Mount Athos, did not hesitate to take even the humblest beings as icons, calling us to venerate them in the same way:

> This blade of grass is an icon; this stone is an icon; and I may embrace it and venerate it since it is filled with the grace of God.[100]

Of course, the error of the iconoclasts must be avoided, for they considered those who venerate icons to be idolaters: it is not matter itself, or the representations in themselves which are venerated in an icon, but the model to whom it refers, or, as is the case here, to God Who is made manifest.

CONTEMPLATIVE RELATIONSHIPS WITH CREATURES

After what has been written above, it can be said that the ideal relationship of man with nature is in part contemplative. Man should see in creation a world of signs and symbols which bring his spirit to God. He should read the *logoi* of the creatures and perceive the divine energies active within them. He should perceive spiritually the relationship of creatures with God and be aware of what the creatures say of God Who manifests Himself in them.

The idea that man is called to contemplate creation is proposed and developed in detail by St Maximos the Confessor. It is also supported by St Gregory of Nyssa[101] and St John of Damascus.[102] And St Joseph the Hesycast, that great spiritual master of our time, spontaneously sees in this the reason why man was created last, as king of all things:

> Finally, God created man like a king over all things, as if he were called to be a spectator in a theatre. [...] All of which the Holy Scripture speaks, all of it was made for man. This is also why man was created last: so that he should see that everything was very good (cf. Gen 1:8, 10, 12, 18, 21, 25) and that he should rejoice and exult in its contemplation.[103]

The creation speaks to us of God through its creatures just as the Holy Scripture speaks of Him through words, and the icons with their forms and colors. St Nicholas (Velimirovich) considers all nature as theology:

> Theology means the word of God, so theology is all or nothing. The whole of nature, that which is above nature, and that which is beneath nature, all these things are theology. Every person and all his parts are theology. Each field and each flower are theology. Sirius and the Milky Way, the nebulae and the meteors are theology. The history of radioactivity and the history of each butterfly, of each grain of sand and each drop of water and all the rays of light are theology.
>
> If the whole of nature is not theology then theology is nothing or nature is nothing. If the whole of nature does not speak of God, who will believe Isaiah or St Paul? If the whole world around us is a desert, what can the voice of a prophet accomplish, weeping for God in the desert? If the whole universe does not speak of God, who can hear the words of a man without contempt.
>
> Consider the lilies of the field: if they tell you nothing of God, then neither would the great riches and wisdom of Solomon speak to you of Him. [...].

> Our generation seeks a sign—a heavenly miracle—to believe. "Show us God," say many of our contemporaries, "And we will believe." [...] We should reply: "Show us rather what is not God!"[104]

According to St Maximos the Confessor, creation, like man, is made up of a soul and an intellect combined with a body with its feelings. Man can perceive it spiritually through its intelligible reality contained in its *logoi* and which reveals God; and he can perceive it in the flesh, simply through its perceptible appearance.

The tree of the knowledge of good and evil spoken of in Genesis (Gen 2:17) represents, for St Maximos, the twofold aspect of creation as it may be seen by man. Knowledge of good corresponds to the spiritual contemplation of perceptible creation. Man comes to know it through the *logoi* it contains, and his spirit is nourished[105] by it through what St Maximos calls "natural contemplation" (*physike theoria*). Knowledge of evil corresponds to the creation considered in the flesh, through its perceptible appearance which beguiles the senses.[106]

In the beginning, Adam was able to choose either of these two ways thanks to his free will. The divine command forbad man to eat of the fruit of the tree of knowledge of good and evil lest he take the second way. Only the first way was in accord with the plan and Will of God. It involves a contemplative approach to nature where God can be seen in every creature and every creature is perceived in God. Creation is then a support, helping man to rise up to God,[107] and allowing man to raise up creation to God in contemplation.

As taught by the entire Orthodox spiritual tradition, contemplation requires a pure spirit and a pure heart free from passions.[108] Then the second degree of spiritual life is opened which can lead man finally to knowledge of God and intimate communion with Him therein. The passions lead man to turn in on himself and see in things nothing beyond their appearance. They prevent the indirect vision of God through His creatures, and, far more so, they block that direct spiritual vision imparted by the Spirit which the Fathers call *theologia*. The passions are founded on the egotistical love of oneself which the Greek Fathers call *philautia*. They are an obstacle to love: the love of God, the love of neighbor and the love of creatures in God whereas contemplation and the Eucharist bear witness to love, and presuppose its presence.

THE EUCHARISTIC USE OF CREATURES

The ideal relationship between man and God is eucharistic: man should return to God with thanksgiving what God has given him. Many Fathers have referred to the praise offered by the first man in Paradise, but St Maximos the Confessor added to this a wonderful description of the eucharistic work to which man was called from the beginning. He writes that man was called to examine the spiritual *logoi* of created beings so as to give them back to God, to give thanks to Him through them and so to turn his spiritual contemplation of nature into a "cosmic liturgy."[109] Man is then at once a gardener (Gen 2:15; cf. 2:5) and a priest of creation. As a gardener he harvests all the *logoi* of beings. As a priest he offers the *logoi* to God Who first gave them, just as the priest at the Liturgy offers bread and wine to God saying: "Thine, of thine own, we offer unto thee in all and for all."[110]

In this light we can see that for St Maximos, Adam's God-given power to name the creatures is the ability to define them according to the *logoi* on which their existence is founded, so as to see God within them and offer them back to God.

As we have seen, God did not forbid man to consume the creatures of the created world. The book of Genesis recounts how God said to Adam and Eve: "Behold, I have given you every seed [...], and every tree whose fruit yields seed [...]; to you it shall be for food" (Gen 1:29); and later he said to Adam: "You may eat food from every tree of the garden" (Gen 2:16). The command to abstain from the fruit of the tree of knowledge of good and evil was given not just that man might retain his contemplative view of creation, but also that his consumption of creatures should be eucharistic. Thus he would avoid a fleshly and passionate perception and consumption of creatures.[111] For this separates them from God and turns them into purely material objects to satisfy man's lust. The eucharistic use of creatures for man is gratitude, thanksgiving, and praise offered to their Creator. It is also an act which sanctifies them, just as in the eucharistic Liturgy, though to a lesser degree. St Irenaeus expresses this briefly and simply: "We offer this to Him, not as if He were in need of it, but to thank Him through His gifts and to hallow all creation."[112]

MAN: THE MEDIATOR BETWEEN NATURE AND GOD

The previous section describes how man may have a contemplative and eucharistic relationship with nature which leads us on to a description of man's mediating function mentioned above. St Gregory of Nyssa explains that man was the last to be brought into the creation after it had been completely made ready for him so that he might be its contemplator. It is in this state that man has the gift from God of mastery over the world. At the same time, through the creatures, man rises up toward God:

> Then God made man appear in this world to be the contemplator of the wonders of the universe and its master. He wishes that their enjoyment should bring knowledge of Him Who had provided them, whilst the grandiose beauty of what he beholds should lead to the ineffable and inexpressible power of the Creator.[113]

To man as the king of creation, the Master delegates a mastery over beings which is expressed particularly in his power to name the creatures.[114] And man is called to perceive God in His creatures and there to contemplate Him, *a descending mediation* between God and the creatures. He is also called raise the creatures up to God, by a unifying contemplation which sees God as their beginning and their end. According to St Maximos the Confessor, he raises the particular *logoi* up to the general *logoi*. And then, in his eucharistic work, he returns the creatures to God, their beginning and their end, with praise and thanksgiving: an *ascending mediation* between the creatures and God.

St Maximos sees man as having yet another call to mediation: to unify all creatures in himself so as to unite them, through himself, to God.[115] This is why man is set by God at the summit and center of creation, to unite it spiritually, then to join it spiritually to God.

St Maximos explains that in the beginning there were different poles in creation which man was to unite.[116] Without man's mediation, these different poles could become oppositions and divisions, and this in fact occurred through the first man's sin.

Once all creation was united, man was to act as mediator by raising it up to God, which, of course, implies that he himself was moving toward God. Then, finally, man was to bring the beings united in himself to participate in his own divinization.[117]

This divine plan is set forth by St Maximos in *Ambiguum* 41:

> The fifth [division] concerns the final creature, like a laboratory in which everything is concentrated, providentially placed above all other beings [...] as a natural mediator of the extremes of all these divisions: man [...], who, centrally placed, is naturally gifted with every power of unification through the correspondence of the various parts of his being with all these extremes. Through this ability, aligned with the cause of the creation of all these divided beings, the way in which the great mystery of the divine plan should be manifest is revealed. The extremes which divide the different beings are brought harmoniously to the good end of their reciprocal unification, going from the closest to the furthest and from the least to the finest through a tension whose end is in God. This is why man is brought in last amongst all beings, as a natural link by placing the parts of his being between the all-embracing extremes. Thus he brings into unity within himself those beings whose nature places a great distance between them. Then, since it is union with God, as first cause, which brings all together, [man], by first uniting his own division then going progressively and in order through all intermediate states as far as God, may reach the limit of the sublime and unifying ascension through all [that is, God] in Whom is no division.[118]

In the *Ambiguum* 7, this calling of man is presented more succinctly, but the mediating role of Adam and his unifying task are clearly stated. The first man appears as he who draws all the beings of creation into himself, so allowing God to be all in all. The body of man is central to this through its nature, common to all perceptible beings, and through its union with the soul which makes possible its own spiritualization.[119]

Man was able to exercise the role of mediation through his bodily nature, but he clearly needed his reason and intellectual powers to accomplish it. This was not the case for any other created being, including the angels since they lack the necessary bodily dimension.

We have already seen that all creatures are objectively linked to God through their *logoi* and the presence within them of the divine energies. So they bear witness to His presence analogically, as the Greek Fathers say, as far as their own nature allows, and praise Him, each in its own way. However, God wished that this should be accomplished consciously in love and freedom which are unique to man amongst all the creatures of the perceptible world. This is why man's mediation was required and why God called him to this task. St Leontios of Neapolis emphasizes man's indispensable mediation:

> Through the heavens, the earth and the sea, through wood and stone and through all the visible and invisible creation I venerate the Creator, Master and Creator of all things. For the creation does not in itself directly venerate the Creator, but it is through my mediation that the heavens tell of the glory of God, and that the Moon and the Sun adore Him. Through my mediation the waters and the rain showers, the dew and the whole creation venerate God and give Him glory.[120]

The contemplative and eucharistic work given to man is essentially one of relationship. It implies that man should not use creation egotistically or just for his own needs. For him, all creatures should always be transparent to God and lead to a relationship with God. In the same way, man should be the means for creatures to relate to God. Such a relationship does not deny the direct and objective relationship of creatures to God, nor does it add anything to this. It assumes their relationship in a free and conscious act of love which recapitulates them.

CONCLUSION

Some modern thinkers believe that the solution to the present ecological crisis lies in questioning basic and fundamental Christian teaching on man's place and role in creation. What troubles them is not man's superiority over creatures nor his power over them, but rather the kind of superiority which is implied and how it is seen, and the type of power and the way it is exercised. For Christians, there is no sense in criticizing the anthropocentric vision of Christianity if it is going to be replaced with a vision centered on nature. Man is then one creature amongst many, living alongside them,[121] and he is drawn into a form of naturalism, or on a religious level, into neo-paganism. Those who propose to place nature at the center are usually inspired by Hinduism or American eco-spirituality linked to the New Age. These are re-hashed versions of Far Eastern religions where all is in everything, all is divine and animals have the same value as man, and man as the animals. The Christian view is anthropocentric, placing man as the mediator; but all this rests on a theocentric foundation. It is quite plain that "The Earth is the Lord's and all that therein is." He is its sole Master for He is its origin, and through His Providence for all His creatures, He is its end. It is also clear that man has this place, not from himself, but through God's good pleasure so that he may fulfill his mission whose end is in God Himself. Basically, this mission is to raise up in contemplation and eucharistic action all creatures to God. Man is to accomplish in knowledge and love that to which all creatures strive unconsciously, instinctively and without unity.

The Christian view can be described as the anthropocentric, a view which, far from setting nature apart and devaluing it, allows its enhancement through man's appointed work to be the mediator between it and God and between God and it. Through his consciousness, his contemplation, and his thanksgiving he brings to it in different measures the blessing of the grace he has received from the Spirit in Christ, which raises it up and transfigures it.

The problem does not lie in the anthropocentric view, where man collaborates with God to enhance nature spiritually, a view strongly promoted by Orthodox theology as synergy. The problem comes from the anthropocentrism which comes from sin and the fall of man, who then takes the place of God and brings all creatures under his sway, and his alone with the aim of profiting from them egotistically. This is an example of a common mistake: to confuse man's original nature with his fallen nature.

To sum up, Orthodox Christianity strongly emphasizes the value of nature's beings since they have a natural and permanent relationship with the Creator. Furthermore, this relationship is truly and permanently clear to the prayerful and contemplative consciousness of man, who bears the responsibility of preserving all creatures and of causing them to flourish, primarily in a spiritual way. The greatness of this calling of man gives him worth for sure. Yet it in no way diminishes the worth of natural creatures. Instead, it recognizes and enhances their worth, raising it through contemplation and eucharistic offering to the highest degree.

Chapter 2

The Sin of Mankind and Its Ecological Consequences

ANCESTRAL SIN

Man was called to cultivate the harmonious relationship which he enjoyed with nature in the beginning, but instead he destroyed it with his ancestral sin. As we have seen, this relationship depends on Man's relationship with God, most especially on his ability to see in creatures the presence of God's plan by means of praise and contemplation and the eucharistic offering of these creatures to God.

According to St Maximos the Confessor, ancestral sin arose in ignorance of God combined with man's beguilement by the perceptible appearances of creatures which promised him sensual pleasure.[1] Ancestral sin was, at the bottom, mankind's separation from God. Man turned away from God to set his desire upon creatures, as independent realities. He then turned inwards to claim these creatures for himself and no longer offered them back to their Creator.

Man's divorce from God through sin thus caused the divorce of man from nature. In appearance, man seemed to become more like the creatures, but in substance man lost touch with their true reality defined by their relationships to God. Man saw nothing in creatures beyond their perceptible appearance, ignoring that God is present in them through His energies and the *logoi* He had placed within them. As St Maximos explains, Adam was beguiled by their apparent beauty and could no longer see beyond it.[2]

Sin led man to see creatures in the wrong light, and this led him to abuse them. This dialectic between ignorance of God and the materialist use of nature for egotistical enjoyment, Saint Maximos describes thus:

> The first man abandoned the movement towards its goal of the energy of the powers in accord with true nature. He fell sick with ignorance of his own origin. Through the counsel of the serpent he came to see himself as god, something from which the word of Divine command had made him swear to abstain. So he became a transgressor, and turning from God, he mingled intimately all his intellectual power with all his sensitivity and drew down upon himself the fractured and death-dealing knowledge of perceptible realities which brings forth the passions. And "he is like the beasts that perish." (Ps 48/49, 13), since he brings forth, seeks and desires the same things as they do; and worse: in his folly he exchanges his natural reason for that which is against nature.
>
> So, insofar as man is drawn to knowing visible realities through his natural senses alone, he binds to himself ignorance of God. The more he tightens this bond of ignorance, the more he is addicted to enjoying the fleshly delights of the material realities which he knows.[3]

THE PASSIONS AT THE ROOT OF THE ABUSE OF CREATURES

Reducing nature to what the senses can perceive to the exclusion of the vision of the spirit (*nous*) leads creatures to be used in a passionate and sensual way.[4] Henceforth man sees the creatures simply as objects for egotistical enjoyment: means of satisfying the passions which have developed in him as a result of his ancestral sin.

According to St Maximos the Confessor, the first of these passions and the mother of all the others is *philautia* or the egotistical love of self. He explains that this fundamental passion is intimately linked to the body and the love which fallen man feels for it.[5] The sensual pleasure which fallen man seeks is first and foremost for his body. He seeks it with passion through creatures which he now sees as instruments of his desires. The most basic passions are those which the Fathers call "bodily": gluttony, where man seeks pleasure through the unfettered consumption of food and drink; lust, where man seeks pleasure through sexual relations which reduce his partner to a consumable object; avarice, where man grasps selfishly at material goods and money; greed, where man seeks always to possess more and more.

The next group of passions in the list drawn up by the Fathers are less bodily in themselves, but are nonetheless closely linked to the body and to material objects: aggression, through which man seeks to gain new goods or to preserve those he already has; fear, of losing what he has or not obtaining what he seeks; sadness, at losing his property or failing to gain something; vanity, through which he preens himself at having more than others; pride, which leads him to compare himself to God and to feel superior to other men.

St Maximos has a vision of these things which may seem very modern, since it is echoed by Freud in his basic concepts of "the principle of pleasure" and "narcissism." The Saint considers that there are two essential tendencies giving rise to the passions which excite fallen man. They are rooted in self-love (*philautia*) and its basic link with the body: seeking pleasure and avoiding discomfort or pain. He can thus distinguish three kinds of passion: the first two kinds spring from each tendency separately, and the third from their combination.[6]

St Maximos sees that this has grave consequences for ethics: it leads naturally to the idea that what gives pleasure is true goodness, and what causes pain or discomfort is evil.[7] This shows why God forbad Adam to touch the tree of the knowledge of good and evil.[8]

Theodore of Mopsuestia and his disciple, St John Chrysostom strongly emphasized how the passions are linked to the fear of death which lies in every man, and how they arouse it. In many cases, the passions are seen, or so we believe, as activities which shield us from death or which fill up our lives before death ends them. They are often the sign of an unhealthy "will to live" or "vital instinct." They are often expressed to protect against menaces or the threat of death. Aggression often fulfills this role: to protect our life or to get what is needed to preserve it. Avarice and its companion, greed, are closely linked to fear, disquiet, or anxiety: the fear of being in need, in danger of illness or of death.

We can see that for man the passions are not simply various paths to the sensual pleasure he seeks to replace the spiritual joy he lost when he parted from God. He also feels they protect him against all that threatens his life once he has rejected the grace which once preserved him perfectly. Moreover, they are, for him, the way to prosper in this world by preserving and increasing his wealth, rather than by prospering spiritually by growing in virtue and the knowledge of God.

THE FIRST TECHNOLOGIES AND THE EFFECTS OF ANCESTRAL SIN

As we have seen, in Paradise man fed himself by harvesting the fruits which nature produced spontaneously; but after man's sin, nature no longer produced these fruits unless it was cultivated.[9] The book of Genesis does indeed make plain that God, in the beginning, gave man the command to cultivate the earth (cf. Gen 2:15), but before man's sin he could accomplish this without hardship[10] (cf. Gen 3:17–18). The Fathers considered that its aim was to make him care for creation and that it had a spiritual dimension.

Once man had sinned, the nature of his work changed. He suffered hardship as he worked: "Then to Adam He said, [...] cursed is the ground in your labors. In toil you shall thou eat from it all the days of your life" (Gen 3:17).

According to the Bible, some of Adam's descendants became blacksmiths to make the tools this work required (Gen 4:22). This is the beginning of the technologies which human reason was to develop. Departing from contemplation, it turned to the perceptible and henceforth worked to develop an ever more complex science linked to the senses,[11] material things,[12] and nature considered apart from God. At first, this science was occult, and led to the practice of magic;[13] but later it took a more rational form to serve as the basis of more advanced technologies.[14]

We now know that even the most advanced science rests on hypotheses which change as time goes by, so that its conclusions are always conjectures and are never completely certain. Kant emphasized that we can only know phenomena—the external aspect of things—and never the things in themselves. Those epistemologists who follow his thought have finished by dissociating scientific knowledge from reality itself. They find that the truth we see in science arises from its internal coherence rather than from its match to reality. It is amazing to see how Clement of Alexandria in the second century finds a double limitation to science: its link to sensations and its conjectural character. He contrasts it to Faith, the only certain knowledge:

> Sensation opens the door to science, whereas faith, after passing over perceptible things, abandons conjecture to hasten to those things which do not deceive but are firm in truth.[15]

St Maximos explains that in the beginning science and technology were of no use:

> In the beginning, man was in no way driven by any of those things beneath him, or around him or after his fashion. To reach perfection he had need of only the one unique thing which leads to Him Who is above him: God. He needed the irresistible movement of the power of loving to the full. Being impassible through grace, he did not give in to the beguilement of those tempting pleasures which arise in the passionate imagination. Since he lacked nothing, he was free from the need of those techniques which are required when need arises. Being wise, he stood through his knowledge above the study of nature. So there was nothing which could hinder the first man from gaining knowledge from God, and nothing which could hinder his freely chosen relationship which was to be perfected through his movement towards God.[16]

St Maximos suggests here that science and technology are signs of fallen man's banishment into the world, and are obstacles to his relationship with God, an idea which St Gregory Palamas takes up:

> The Evil One, who always seeks cunningly to turn us way from what is highest, gives birth to enchantments in our souls and, almost without fail, binds them with those bonds so dear to men full of vanity: he shows us a deep and varied perspective, the vast number of things we

> may know, just as to others he proposes riches or vainglory and fleshly pleasures, so that we should pass our whole life in seeking them and not have the strength firmly to pursue the education which purifies the soul [and brings it to knowledge of the mysteries of God]. Even the beginning of these things is hidden from a man given to the love of vain philosophy and wholly absorbed by its figures and theories.[17]

St Isaac the Syrian stresses the link between science and its techniques with the body and all the cares which go with its needs. He shows how they are substitutes for faith in Providence, and haunt man with various fears from which he vainly imagines they can deliver him.

> When knowledge is stamped with love of the body, it is attracted to the following things: riches, vainglory, elegant clothes, bodily comfort and a taste for rational wisdom which is well adapted to the way of this world. It is pleased by the abundance of new inventions in science and technology and by everything which helps to glorify the body in this visible world. All this means that it is opposed to Faith as we have said and explained above. We say that it is a "bare knowledge" (*psile gnosis*) since it has been stripped of any memory of God and gives birth to the weakness of an unreasonable spirit since it is ruled by the body and cares for nothing but this world. Knowledge at this level is unaware that there is a spiritual Power, an invisible Governor Who guides man, and a divine Providence which cares for him and looks after him in a perfect way. This knowledge thinks that every good thing which comes to man, everything which saves him from possible harm, everything which preserves us from all the perils and dangers which threaten us, openly or secretly, and are found in our nature, arises solely from our own efforts and our natural genius. In this state, knowledge believes it can boast of being universal providence itself. It agrees with those who believe that there is no [higher] ruler of the visible world. However, it is impossible for it to surmount its disquiet and continual fear for the body. It is spineless and haunted by sadness, despair, the fear of demons, cowardice before men, rumors of brigands, tales of deadly deeds, worries over illness, fear of poverty and lack of necessities, fear of death and suffering, fear of dangerous animals and storms at sea, and many other such

things which threaten us every hour of the day and the night. It cannot lay its cares upon God with the confidence which comes from Faith in Him. This is why it never ceases to ponder over works and to calculate everything; and when all its efforts fail through some circumstance and it sees that its secret plans [will not succeed], it fights those men who are in its way and opposes them.[18]

When knowledge cleaves to the love of the body, it gathers up the following provisions: wealth, vainglory, [honor], adornment, rest of the body, [special means to guard the body's nature from adversity], assiduity in rational wisdom, such as is suitable for the governance of the world and which gushes forth the novelties of inventions, the arts, sciences, [doctrines], and all other things which crown the body in this visible world. Among the properties of this knowledge belong those which are opposed to faith, which we have enumerated above. This is called shallow knowledge, for it is naked of all concern for God. And because it is dominated by the body, it introduces into the mind a rational impotence, and its concern is totally for this world. This measure of knowledge does not reckon that there is any noetic power and hidden steersman over a man, nor any Divine care that shelters and takes concern for him. It takes no account of God's providential governance; but on the contrary, it attributes to a man's diligence and his methods every good thing in him, his rescue from what harms him, and his natural ability to avert the plights and many adversities that secretly and manifestly accompany our nature. This degree of knowledge presumes that all things are by its own providence, like those men who assert that there is no Divine governance of visible things. Nevertheless, it cannot be without continual cares and fear for the body. There fore it is a prey to faintheartedness, sorrow, despair, fear of the demons, trepidation before men, the rumor of thieves and the report of murders, anxiety over illnesses, concern over want and the lack of necessities, fear of death, fear of sufferings, of wild beasts, and other similar things which make this knowledge like a sea turbulent by great waves at every hour of the night and day. For knowledge does not know how to cast its care upon God through the confident trust of faith in Him; wherefore in all things that concern it, it is constantly engaged in devising devices and clever contrivances. But when in some instance the modes of its contrivances prove fruitless, it strives with men as tough they had hindered and opposed it, since it does not see in this the mystical hand of providence.[19]

DISORDER SPREADS THROUGH NATURE AND BECOMES PART OF IT

Sin brought great disorder into human nature which the Fathers have described extensively. Starting from the spiritual realm, it spread to the psychological and physical spheres. It brought about many kinds of sickness marked by their unnatural (relative to our original nature) operation: instabilities, various disorders, conflict, and divisions, and for the body, corruption, and finally death.[20]

St Gregory of Nyssa shows how man's spirit, originally a mirror of divine beauty, which is order and harmony, becomes ugly. When it turns from God it becomes disordered and discordant, and passes its ugliness on to nature, which is a "mirror of the mirror." This discord and disorder, nature then passes on to matter of which it is the form and organizational principle. He shows also that this process reverses, so that the evil imparted to matter infects nature which then infects the spirit.[21]

St Gregory of Nyssa and St Maximos the Confessor clearly see sexual reproduction (which appeared after the ancestral sin) as a biological cause and multiplier of the transmission of the effects of ancestral sin from generation to generation in the human race. It could be described in modern scientific terms as a genetic factor.[22]

Man, who was the first to be infected by evil, spreads it throughout the whole creation. Then he, in turn, is re-infected in a different way and for various reasons:

1) He is contaminated since he is a microcosm who contains all that constitutes nature and synthesizes all the natural realms.
2) Because God gave him power over creation by making him its king, creation depends on him. So he draws all creatures down with him in his fall. St Makarios of Egypt goes further, saying that by worshiping the demons, man delvers into their power all the creatures which he should have offered to God in his Eucharist:

> Imagine a king with riches at his disposal and retainers who submit to him in service. It then happens that he is taken by his enemies and bound in

> captivity. Once he has been taken prisoner and sent into exile, his retainers and household are obliged to follow him. In the same way, Adam was created pure by God to serve Him Who gave him all the other creatures as his servants. He was established as lord and king of all creatures. When the word of evil drew nigh to converse with him, at first he listened outwardly with his ears; but then it penetrated within him through his heart and robbed him of all his substance. When he was taken captive, all creation, which was at his service and obeyed him, was taken captive too. For it was through him that death came to reign over every soul, and by his disobedience that the image of Adam was entirely blotted out. Thus did men go astray and went so far as to worship demons. For the fruits of the earth, created good by God, they offered to demons. They set on their altars bread, wine, oil and animals, and even sacrificed their own sons and daughters to demons. (cf. Ps 105/106, 37)[23]

3) Because man, by turning from God, no longer watches over nature, and is no longer the master of natural beings.
4) Because his treatment of nature, in which his life unfolds, has its effects on the state of nature.

St Maximos the Confessor sums up these different points thus:

> Man received from God by grace the power, as master of the world, to do as he would with what God had created. Abusing this power, he acted against nature, and imparted to himself, and to all the cosmos, the present degradation.[24]

So the disorder which came from sin did not just change the relationship of man with nature, but became part of nature itself.

In the writings of St Athanasius of Alexandria there is a passage which could suggest that apart from man, creation remained untouched: "None of the beings in nature fell into error as regards knowledge of God save man alone. The Sun, the Moon, the sky, the stars, the water, the ether were untroubled in their course. Knowing the Word, their creator and king, they remained as they were created."[25] St Athanasius is here referring to sin: all the Fathers affirm that man alone is to blame since he alone has free will. This does not mean that other creatures do no harm,[26] nor that they are unaffected by evil,[27] but that they are not responsible for it and cannot be blamed.[28] Their untroubled course and the fact that they remain as they were created are of ethical and spiritual significance rather than physical or material.

According to the Bible and the Fathers, man is not the only cause of this disorder. When he lost the grace which united him with God, he ceased to be the king of the creation which God had entrusted to him. He abandoned it to the Devil who then became the "prince of this world."

Evil entered nature in various forms to which the Bible refers symbolically: "Then to Adam He said, [...] cursed is the ground in your labors. In toil [...] both thorns and thistles it shall bring forth for you" (Gen 3:17–18). The prophet Isaiah also recounts the destructive effects of man's sin upon nature:

> The earth mourns and the inhabited earth is ruined; the lofty of the earth mourn. The earth acts lawlessly because of its inhabitants, for they transgressed the law and changed the ordinances, the everlasting covenant. Therefore a curse shall devour the earth, because those who dwell in it sinned. Therefore the inhabitants of the earth shall be poor, and few people will be left. The wine shall mourn, the vine shall mourn, and all the merry- hearted will groan. (Isa 24:4–7)

There is a very ancient text, found in the liturgical texts of the 8-tone cycle of the Orthodox Church, the *Paracletic*. It is noteworthy that this text describes how, when man fell, the pollution of the earth, the waters and the air were caused by his sin, for this was at a time when such things were slight and almost imperceptible compared to what they are today:

> I have become the jest of the demons, the disgrace of the human race, the grief of all the righteous, the affliction of the holy angels, *the pollution of the air, the earth and the water;* I have soiled my soul, my body and my spirit; I am become the enemy of God by my senseless deeds: Alas, O Lord, I have sinned against Thee, I have sinned, grant me pardon.[29]

NATURE IS NO LONGER ENTIRELY GOOD

Nature, in the beginning, was entirely good, as the book of Genesis insists at every stage of the creation, stating: "And God saw that it was very good." However, evil is now present there in many forms and to various extents. There are destructive elements, both biological and physical, which bring sickness, corruption, and death, along with violence (of the elements and the animals) and conflict between species and between individuals or elements of the animal, vegetable, and mineral worlds.

Divine Providence respects man's freedom, even when he abuses it, with evil effects, which is why it does not hinder him from bringing evil on nature and spreading it everywhere. Still, it does not allow the world to slide rapidly down the slope to destruction in accord with its corrupted state. Providence "creates a certain order in the midst of disorder,"[30] preserving a little of the original order. We may see this in God's thought after the flood as the book of Genesis recounts:

> Then the Lord thought it over and said, "I will never again curse the earth because of man's works, although the mind of man is diligently involved with evil things from his youth; nor will I again destroy every living thing as I have done. While the earth remains, seedtime and harvest, cold and heat, summer and spring shall not cease by day and night." (Gen 8:21–22)

and the words of God to Noah and his sons:

> Behold, I am establishing My covenant with you and with your seed after you, and every living creature with you: the birds, the cattle, and all the wild animals, of all that came out of out of the ark with you. Thus I will establish My covenant with you, and never again shall all flesh be cut off by the waters of the flood; nor shall there ever be a flood to destroy the earth. (Gen 9:9–11)

God speaks to them also to confirm the lordship of man over all living creatures: God blesses Noah and his sons, saying:

> Increase and multiply, and fill the earth, and have dominion over it. For the dread and fear of you shall be upon all the wild animals of the earth,

> all the birds of heaven, all that move upon the earth, and all the fish of the sea. I have put them under your authority. (Gen 9:1–2)

St John Chrysostom teaches that divine Providence sets limits to the Universe and a brake on its decline. Its opposing forces are held together to prevent its destruction:

> In the universe [...] each element remains in its place, held as if with a bridle, bound by the will of the Creator who keeps it within its limits; and so this opposition of the elements brings peace to the whole universe. Yes, even the blind will see, and the senseless understand that they were made and are upheld by divine Providence, which binds them within their limits. Before the sight of such a whole with such great beauty, and so carefully arranged despite the collision of opposing elements which nonetheless endure, who could be so senseless or stupid as not to reason thus? Unless the hand of Providence upheld the mass of all these bodies of the Universe to prevent its dissolution, it could not remain or last.[31]

St Symeon the New Theologian explains, for his part, that following man's sin, the order of nature is reversed, against itself and against man:

> When Adam was put out of Paradise, the whole creation which had been raised up by God from nothing, when it saw him, refused to submit any more to the transgressor. The Sun no longer wished to shine, the moon would have remained hidden, the stars were unwilling to be seen by him, the springs would have dried up, the rivers would not flow, the air thought to enclose itself and no longer give breath to the rebel. The wild beasts and all the animals of the earth saw him bereft of his former glory and, disdaining him, turned all their violence against him. The sky was ready to fall upon him, and the earth hurried to throw him off its back.

God then intervened so that man might be preserved, and later be saved:

> What did God do then, He Who had formed the Universe and then created Adam? Since He had known from before the beginning of the

> world that this man would disobey His command, and as He had predetermined that his birth to a new life and his renewal would depend on the birth in the flesh of His only Son and God, what did He do? He restrained all these creatures by an action of His own power. With mercy and goodness He holds back the onslaught of this alliance of the creatures.[32]

According to St Maximos the Confessor, the created world is not affected in its essence (its *logos* remains the same), but in its mode of existence. Its *tropos* no longer conforms to its *logos*.

Amongst Western thinkers, Pascal, like all the members of the circle of Port Royal, was imbued with the thought of the Greek Fathers. He was therefore clearly aware that nature is double. Though it is marked by the consequences of sin, yet it still retains something of its original nature.[33]

There are also those who believe that nature is evil and that it is up to man to make it good. This applies also to man himself, who, says Hobbes, "is a wolf for man." The task of the state is then to create a legal framework which puts an end to "the natural state," where men, given over to their egotism, their passions, and their native violence are always in conflict, the strong seeking to dominate and exploit the weak.[34] A similar idea can be found in the works of Freud. For him, society, through its laws and morality, seeks to limit and regulate sexual desire which has no rule other than the pursuit of pleasure; likewise aggression, which is as much a part of nature as sexual desire.[35]

As regards nature itself, some thinkers consider that at the bottom it is wild, man's task being to subdue it and tame it. For them, civilization is set up, as it were, against nature so as to tame it as if it were a wild beast. Thus in the humanist system of Descartes, the role of technology is "to make man master and owner of nature" by his skill in mastering forces at least as great as nature's through the masterly harnessing and direction of its own energies.

There are also those who think that nature is good, and should be respected, protected, and completely preserved in its present state. They think that it represents a standard for all to follow, and that any evil we may meet is the simply the fruit of human activity and of society. This is the idea of Jean-Jacques Rousseau who affirms that man is born good but is corrupted by society.[36] There is a whole current of eighteenth-century thought which exalts the virtues of nature seen as being in itself beautiful, pure, and innocent.[37] Today, these ideas have been adopted by part of the ecological movement, whose politics, like those of all the left, are based on the thoughts of Rousseau. This leads to a form of ecology which preaches the respect of nature, even in its faults, and takes it as the standard for human behavior. This is found even in certain Christian circles of which, for example, Pierre Rahbi is a typical representative.

Another school which has an entirely positive view of nature comes from sources of a very different kind which deify and idolize it. From a Christian point of view, it is neo-pagan. A great variety of religious or pseudo-religious practices go with it. They may be pantheist or animist, where the world and all things in it are taken to be divine, God or gods being incarnate in various creatures, or in the spirits which dwell within them. Various spiritualist groups share these views, such as those in the New Age movement which are especially inspired by Hinduism and Buddhism.

In the United States especially, ecological groups have embraced these ideas, giving rise to an ecology which tries to be more spiritual than political. It is sometime called ecospirituality. This kind of ecology has infected certain Christian groups who appropriate certain parts of Christian theology to suit its agenda; for instance, the theology of the Incarnation, or the Orthodox theology of the divine energies, twisting them into meanings they never had. In some Christian circles, ecology can even be treated as a substitute for theology. This leads to a veritable cult of nature, of natural products, of a green diet, and of vegan food, whose pseudo-religious character is obvious and often leads to the birth of sects. Nature is seen in a completely positive way. Specifically, they go further, treating the goodness of nature as an absolute.

The Christian position differs from all these schools of thought. Nature in its present state is seen neither as something purely negative to be corrected, nor as something entirely positive to be preserved at all costs. Still less is it an absolute reality to be venerated for itself, or a standard by which all else should be measured.

Nature is a mixed reality which in its essence preserves something of its original perfection. Through what St Maximos the Confessor calls the *logoi,* it basically retains a relationship with God in its beginning and its end. Some of this perfection remains in its organization, though it cannot be identified with

God or taken as divine; for it is also marked by the imprint of the sin of man, and the action of devils and demons which infects it with evil. This evil can be seen, for example, in the violence and destruction wrought by the unfettered elements, in the violence and cruelty which govern the relationships of animals and in the corrupting and death-dealing powers of certain bacteria and viruses which cause man and living creatures to suffer and die.

Yet Christianity continues to proclaim, in a prayer which the Orthodox faithful recite several times per day, that the Holy Spirit, God, "is everywhere present and fillest all things."[38]

It is, of course, true that the divine energies remain present and active in the world; but since the fall, they are no longer properly and fully received by man and the creatures for whom he is mediator. For the Fathers, God is present and active in His grace, which is the gift of His energies to man and the world. For man to benefit fully, and to pass this on to the creatures, he must receive it fully and freely. For God fully respects his freedom to accept them or to refuse, to open himself up to them or to shut them out, to live united and in conformity with them, or in discord, separation, and opposition to them.

It is true that all creatures retain their essential relationship with God through the *logoi* within them, but here St Maximos the Confessor makes an important distinction: between the *logos* and the *tropos*. Every being remains unchanging in its essential definition and its fundamental relationship with God as origin and end of its being; but its *tropos*, or mode of existence is subject to change. Sin and the fall brought creatures a new mode of existence which no longer accords fully with their *logoi*. Though certain modern commentators on St Maximos do not realize it, the *tropos* is not simply defined by a personal attitude, good or evil, of the one who chooses toward his *logos* but also involves an objective change in the state of creatures.[39] St Maximos teaches that after the fall of man into sin, all creatures exist in accordance with a fallen *tropos*. It is not totally evil, but only in part. Man cannot set this to rights and restore its ideal state except through the grace given by Christ, and which, as a mediator, he can impart to other creatures, to each in its own measure.

Christianity teaches that man should approach his relationship to nature with discernment. He should respect it, maintain it, cultivate it, and make all the good to be found there to flower. He should struggle with all the evil it contains and uproot it: sickness, and all else which can harm its goodness; and he should guard it against the risk of partial or total self-destruction which could also threaten his own existence.

NATURE'S FALLEN STATE: THE RESPONSIBILITY OF ALL

The Bible and the Fathers strongly emphasize the responsibility of our first ancestors, Adam and Eve, for the fall which affected all humanity, and through humanity, all the creation. They were the prototypes of humanity, and the sin with which they infected their own nature affected what then was all of human nature, and so was transmitted to all their descendants.

Unlike Western Tradition, so strongly influenced by St Augustine, Eastern Tradition considers that the descendants of Adam and Eve do not bear the personal guilt of their ancestors, but simply the consequences of their fall. This is why the East speaks of "ancestral sin" or "the sin of the first parents" rather than "original sin." This notion was developed by the followers of St Augustine to become the doctrine of inherited sin and guilt.[40]

Nonetheless, the Greek Fathers consider that by their own personal sins, the descendants of Adam and Eve reproduce and confirm the error of first ancestors.[41] In this way, they not only preserve its effects but spread them out through all human nature and the whole creation. St Paul writes: "through one man sin entered the world, and death through sin" (Rom 5:12), and that "death reigned from Adam [...] even over those who had not sinned according to the likeness of the transgression of Adam" (Rom 5:14); but he also writes: "death spread to all men, because all sinned" (Rom 5:12). So why did the fault of one single person lead to the condemnation of all nature? St John Chrysostom replies: "The first men sinned, and through their disobedience they brought in slavery. And those who came into the world after these events, ratified this enslavement through their own sins."[42]

Chapter 3

How Did We Reach the Present Situation?

Ecological problems are recent problems. As mentioned in Chapter 1, some writers have blamed Christianity for the way nature has been exploited; but the danger to nature did not arise until the twentieth century and only became serious in the twentieth-first century. As we will see, this was mainly caused by the development of technologies based on science. This development, however, grew out of a new concept of God, man, and nature, foreign to traditional religious concepts.

THE NEW PARADIGM OF THE RENAISSANCE

The scientific enterprise grew out of ideas of nature and mankind's relationship to it which appeared during the Renaissance. These ideas developed further in the seventeenth century and were generally adopted in the century of "Lumières" (the Enlightenment). The Western world, where the ecological crisis first arose, had a different view of nature in the Middle Ages. Nature was seen from the all-pervasive Christian viewpoint as being in some way sacred and symbolic, something well illustrated by Romanesque art.

With the coming of the Renaissance to Europe in the sixteenth century, humanism became predominant in every sphere with its consequences: naturalism, rationalism, and individualism.

Humanism

Humanism is the adulation of man considered in himself and for himself. When humanism does not actually deny God, it confines Him to the attic and affirms man's total autonomy in His face. It has an anthropocentric vision of the world which replaces the earlier theocentric vision, so that God is no longer a reference, but man becomes the measure of everything. Nature has no more its reference in God, but in man, who now defines its meaning, its value, and its use. As Descartes wrote in the seventeenth century, man becomes "master and owner of nature." Rejecting his God-given task as the steward of creation, he uses his power to dominate nature, usurping that which belongs to God the Creator and His Providence and treating the world as his own property to be exploited.

Naturalism

The Renaissance is so deeply marked by naturalism that it is often defined as a return to Greek antiquity and a return to nature, the two being linked. By centering everything on man and excluding God, humanism brings everything down a purely naturalistic level. The supernatural is excluded or minimized as much as possible. Renaissance art rejects the symbolic character of medieval art in its representations of man and nature. Even religious art represents Christ, His Mother, and the saints and all the spiritual events of the New Testament in a purely naturalistic way. For their representations of Christ or the Mother of God, the painters and sculptors used human models without any thought for their spiritual qualities. Raphael, for instance, used the faces of his mistresses in his depictions of the Mother of God. Nature was shown as the sole origin of her qualities and resources. Thus she loses all her holiness and all that is spiritual. In one way, naturalism seems to enhance the value of nature, even to excess. This is what gives it its name. Yet in another way, it degrades nature by depriving it of its link to the transcendent which is what gives it its value.

Rationalism

Although the path of rationalism was prepared by the scholastics of the Middle Ages, it was the Renaissance which raised reason to be the main source of human knowledge. The spirit and intellect, the faculties which contemplate supernatural realities, were demeaned. In the seventeenth century, this troubled Pascal. He felt that intuitive knowledge, through the heart, spirit, and intellect, was not only threatened, but even rejected by some of his contemporaries. In one famous "Pensée" (Thought) he insists not simply on the possibility of such knowledge, but on its necessity and superiority to what reason can provide. For reason itself cannot be the source of the axioms which are its own foundation.[1]

The esteem given to reason and the rational approach to phenomena led to the growth of a philosophy which had no need of the theology of which it was once the servant. During the seventeenth century it also encouraged the rise of the sciences which form part of it, as shown in the *Discours de la méthode* of Descartes. Later each science in turn became independent and developed autonomously.

By adopting naturalism and all that goes with it, man abandons all reference to the supernatural in his explanations of nature. Instead, he seeks to understand it in itself alone by reason alone. This contributes to the de-spiritualization of nature and to the strengthening of naturalism.

The "Copernican" revolution, started by Copernicus and continued by Kepler, Galileo, and Newton displaced the center of rotation of the Solar System from the Earth to the Sun. This was a striking break with the past. The knowledge drawn from science was no longer in accord with men's experience and perception of nature, and this break was to be magnified greatly as science advanced. Bachelard, who investigated the epistemology of the development of a scientific mentality and the progress of science, concluded that this involved it in an ever-growing rupture with what he termed "primordial experience."[2] The scientific method is a method of negation which Bachelard called "The philosophy of No." Henceforth man knows something other than what he perceives, and perceives something other than what he knows.

Man's knowledge of nature has become ever more abstract. More and more it is linked to mathematics and expressed in equations and formulae which are the result of calculation and permit further calculations. Science, in this philosophy, is what is quantifiable. All that is qualitative in nature is excluded and its symbolical dimension is systematically rejected.

Individualism

A consequence of the humanism of the Renaissance is the exaltation of the individual. In art this is shown by the importance accorded to the artist as an original creator. This is seen in a striking way in the philosophy of Descartes in the seventeenth century. His famous epithet: "I think therefore I am" sets up the "I" as the unique source and criterion of true knowledge, and even of the self and of the world.

Individualism brought in the age of "every man for himself." The resulting competition led to the capitalism which was to develop in the eighteenth century, and consequently to a weakening of the sense of community and of solidarity.

The Conquest of the New World

The Renaissance was also the time when the conquest of the New World began: India, America, Oceania, etc. This conquest sprang from the desire of European States to increase their power by gaining new lands. These could be exploited and their produce sold for economic benefit. This, without doubt, changed the way Europeans saw nature: they could see it as a renewable source of goods to be exploited and sold. Comparing the mentalities of the conquerors and the conquered in these new lands, it is plain that the first were totally unscrupulous as regards nature, whilst their victims nourished a deep respect for natural creatures through a profound sense of their sacred character.[3]

The Dualism of Soul and Body

Christianity sees the human being as single and undivided, rejecting the dualism of Plato and his gnostic imitators of the first centuries.[4] However Descartes revived this idea of the dualism of soul and body. He reasoned that he could be certain of his existence as a thinking subject, and went on to identify himself, "a thinking substance," with his soul. Only later does his reasoning lead him to the certainty that he has a body, which, however, does not appear to him as being indispensable.[5] Later still, and only after becoming certain of the existence of God, he becomes certain of the existence of the world.[6]

Dualism is not simply linked to Descartes's own thought. It also corresponds to a tendency which became common from the seventeenth century in certain strands of Western Christian spirituality. These were marked by a disdain for the body, which was crudely reduced to the flesh and its passions, and led to extreme forms of bodily mortification.

Setting the body apart from the soul, even to the point of separation and devaluation, had a sure effect on the relationship of man to nature. The body is part of nature and nature a dimension of the body, which sums it up and synthesizes it when man is seen as a microcosm. But the man who adopts the dualistic view feels less close to nature and is not at one with her, caring less for her destiny. He sees her as a reality completely external to what he is, a lesser reality of lesser worth, a reality, which even if not despised and ignored, needs no respect or care or cultivation.

Bodies as Mechanisms

Descartes (1596–1650) considered that animals have no souls and are simply machines.[7] This theory of "animal-machines" is another step toward the de-spiritualization of the world. It advances the idea that creatures, being mere objects, can be used by man without scruple as he wishes as means to an end or as products for consumption.

This mechanistic conception of nature developed over the following centuries with only feeble competition from "vitalism." Its effect was to deprive nature of its qualitative dimension, and to deprive each being of its unity and identity by reducing everything to a structure of different elements.

God as the Absent Watchmaker

The philosophers of this period and those which followed no longer thought of God as the one who reveals himself and is seen by faith, but as a supreme being which reason must postulate to explain the organization of the world. Calvin (1509–1564) saw him as an architect; Galileo (1564–1642) and Leibniz (1646–1715) as a mathematician; Voltaire (1694–1778) as a surveyor, or, like Newton (1643–1727), as a watchmaker. God's function is essentially to conceive all things and to set them in order, as required by this concept of a mathematical and mechanical world with no soul. This abstract, impersonal God has no direct relationship with men nor yet with the other beings of nature. He is simply invoked to justify, *a priori*, the rational order of the Universe, and for some he can disappear once he has set the whole thing in motion.[8]

CONFIRMATION BY THE PHILOSOPHY OF THE ENLIGHTENMENT

The philosophers of the enlightenment, d'Alembert, Voltaire, Diderot, and the rest, confirmed and developed the revolution in thought brought in by the Renaissance, introducing ideas which were openly anti-religious.

- Theism was accepted by some philosophers, but their god was abstract and far off. This god was far from the God of the Christians, and religion was no longer seen in its original etymological sense as that which binds man to God and God to man (Latin: *religare*), but as a mass of superstitions to be suppressed and destroyed.
- Atheism was frequently proposed as the foundation from which naturalism and materialism logically develop. For example, Diderot writes: "The naturalists are those who in no way accept God, but who believe that there is simply a material substance. [...] A naturalist in this sense is the same as an atheist, a materialist, etc."[9]
- Man is affirmed to be the absolute center of reference. "Man is the unique point from which all things must start, and to which all things must return" says Diderot in his usual way.[10]
- Man is set against God, especially against the personal God of the Christians.
- Reason is set up as the chief source of knowledge: "If I deny my reason, I no longer have a guide," wrote Diderot.[11] Reason opposes Faith, both in philosophy and in the sciences.[12] Buffon, for example, rejects the idea that divine intervention can explain what science cannot, and *a fortiori* what science can already explain. Any reference to religion is dismissed as coming from darkened minds and superstition.
- The individual is valued more than the community. The individual is exalted as the source of all thought and as perfectly free to define his own behavior. Tolerance is valued so highly as to justify moral and ethical relativism, bereft of any absolute value. In economics, John Locke defends the idea that all property is private and individual, thus laying a foundation for budding capitalism.

Rousseau and Bernadin de Saint Pierre exalt nature which they see as an absolute good. They see society as the source of its degradation, a position which seems close to modern ecological thought and could even be considered as its foundation. The extreme optimism of these thinkers arises from illusions as we have shown above. Their naturalism makes nature an absolute and rejects its spiritual side: the presence of God's active providence, which gives it its value. Ethics are, in a certain sense, denied, since it is the spontaneous tendencies of nature, instincts, and emotions which these thinkers see as defining good behavior.[13]

The enlightenment's rationalization of our perception of the world is compensated by sentiment. It is no longer compensated, far less surpassed, by the spirit (or intellect) in its contemplation of beings, open to transcendence and symbolic meaning. This tendency was exacerbated in the following century by romanticism, which returns to individualism, making it the subject's center of reference, so that he then sees nature simply in the light of the emotions and feelings of the moment.

THE CRUCIAL ROLE OF MODERN TECHNOLOGY

In traditional societies nature was not much exploited since their technology was too primitive. Over the centuries, of course, it gradually improved, but only slowly. It was at the end of the nineteenth century especially that technologies were developed on the basis of scientific knowledge, acquiring ever greater power from the energies they mastered, from coal, oil, gas, nuclear fission, and electricity.

The capitalist economy, which was born in the previous century, had now developed so much that it could take them up as its instruments of economic exploitation. It was no longer a question of satisfying the basic needs of mankind, but of maximizing profit as much as possible. This implied the unlimited production of more and more articles far beyond people's needs and without any care for them. Advertising and fashion created artificial wants. Useless updates and built-in obsolescence helped force customers to replace goods which had been designed to wear out or which had become obsolete through the programmed development of the technology on which they relied.

All this greatly encouraged the exploitation of nature.

The desire to raise crop yields has given rise to intensive farming, and led to its industrialization. Huge amounts of artificial fertilizer and pesticides, supplied by industry, are used. The farmer gets trapped in a vicious circle. He must invest in equipment, fertilizer, and chemicals to protect his crop so as to get greater yields. He must produce more and more to finance his investment, but overproduction may lead to the destruction of the crops which cannot be sold.

Fossil fuels—coal, gas, and oil—have been widely used in many ways, in industry, for transport, and for heating. They emit huge amounts of exhaust, which change the environment, pollute the earth, and contaminate plants, animals, and mankind. Some of the materials produced from coal and oil can be specially polluting, such as non-biodegradable plastics which have spread everywhere.

Since all these processes described above have continued to develop, they have led to six serious consequences for nature, some of which are irreversible:

- The exhaustion of natural resources and fossil fuels.
- The pollution of the air, water, and the earth.
- The disturbance of those processes which ensure the survival and reproduction of species.
- The consequent disappearance of certain plant and animal species.
- Global warming due to the release of greenhouse gases with the consequent climate change. This leads to changes in the soil, in ecosystems and the plants and animals linked to them. There is an increase in natural catastrophes—heatwaves, storms, hurricanes, and floods—so that life becomes harder in those parts of the world which they affect the most.
- The world's beauty is spoilt by non-biodegradable waste.

All these things lead to serious consequences for humanity, especially the increase in illnesses provoked by pollution, such as cancer, allergies, and infection from bacteria resistant to antibiotics. There is also impoverishment, famine, and exile for those who inhabit regions which environmental change has made inhospitable. In this respect it is obvious that ecological problems are not just problems for nature, but also for humankind dwelling therein whose quality of life is intimately linked to the state of nature.

All these subjects have been extensively studied elsewhere and are well known, so there is no point in us dwelling on them further.

THE FOUNDATION OF SCIENTIFIC AND TECHNOLOGICAL ADVANCE

We may ask why it was not until the nineteenth century that science and technology began to advance rapidly rather than developing much earlier.

The Removal of Spiritual Resistance to Technological Development

It is evident that in all civilizations said to be "traditional" rather than "modern" there is a certain resistance to the development of science and technology which has, in a broad sense, mainly spiritual roots.[14]

The Birth and Growth of Capitalism

There is a similar resistance to the development of capitalism. "Chrematistics," the art of using money to make more, was condemned by Aristotle.[15] Medieval Scholastics, inspired by Aristotle, gave moral rules to the Catholic Church which were given the force of law in society. They forbad Christians to lend at interest (the basis of capitalism) and only allowed it for certain minorities whose field of action was limited.

As Max Weber showed, it was Protestantism which was partly the cause of the rise of capitalism.[16] Freed from Roman Catholic ethics, it promoted individualism and developed a most secular mentality which finally led to the blossoming of capitalism in the eighteenth century.[17] As Marx demonstrated, it was further developed by an emerging class, the bourgeoisie, which ended by taking power from the nobility. This class had as its main goal the acquisition, conservation, and transmission of a material fortune, and the limitless increase of its wealth. Thus the development of the technologies used by modern industry, and the distribution and consumption of its products enabled by the modern economy, is intimately linked to the development of capitalism.

The Reign of Rationalism

Modern technology rests upon the modern scientific method which was developed from the rationalism of the Renaissance alongside humanism and was fortified by the teachings of what is called "the Enlightenment" in the eighteenth century. Rational knowledge became steadily more scientific[18] until it came to be seen as the main way to knowledge of a reality reduced to nature. In the nineteenth century, scientism, an atheist and humanist creed,[19] took it to be the highest form of knowledge. Along with rationalism, which took on an extreme and totalitarian form at that time, science was seen as the only way to know reality. Thus Hegel's affirmation of the identity of the rational and the real—"what is real is rational and what is rational is real"—manages to exclude from reality anything which the reason cannot know.

Rationalism, closely linked to naturalism, finally deprived nature in the Western mind of any spiritual quality or symbolic function. The relations between man and nature lost the dimension of contemplation, since nature was now thought to be an independent and purely material entity, whilst intuitive and spiritual knowledge was despised along with its organ, the spirit or intellect, *nous* in Greek and *intellectus* in Latin. Such knowledge was not just seen as useless, but harmful to the development of objective knowledge. The approach of traditional societies to nature was rejected. Nature was no longer to be studied so as better to live with her and to rise above her spiritually. Instead, she was to be dominated as Descartes prescribed clearly in his *Discours de la méthode*: "To become master and owner of nature," something which modern technology fully achieves.

The Myth of Progress and the Omnipotence of Technology

Christianity is not concerned with the progress of society as such, since Christ declared that His kingdom is not of this world. Christians see spiritual progress as what gives meaning to each person's life. The Christian strives steadily to bring death to "the old man" and to replace him with "the new man." To this end the passions are mortified and their opposing virtues developed. They seek the salvation given by Christ, and through this to progress to deification.

For the philosophers of the enlightenment and their heirs in the nineteenth and twentieth centuries, the idea of progress is external. It no longer lies within the personal being but in the community, and is measured by what one has, not what one is.

Traditional societies, their community and all that goes with it are usually basically conservative. They tend to value what is ancient and are suspicious of change and novelty, which they resist.[20] All scholars agree that the idea of progress is recent. Bacon was probably its first exponent, linking it closely to science and technology,[21] a link which it retains today.

Progress first aims at an improvement of knowledge, a task entirely entrusted to science. The founder of positivism, Auguste Comte, believed that the progress of science was the measure of all human progress. In his "theory of the three states," the age of science which follows the age of theology and the age of metaphysics is the highest, which allows humanity to fulfill itself.[22] Comte wished to erect science as a religion replacing what went before, with its own priests, its own catechism,[23] and its own morality. He believed that science, as it developed, would guarantee the happiness of humanity by answering all its questions and fulfilling all its needs. Henceforth progress was identified with technology, and the philosophers who taught it came quickly to believe that this would make man all-powerful over the world.

Closely linked to the modern idea of progress is the idea that man should do anything which is possible with no ethical limit, just whatever his technology allows. This idea that to do all that is feasible is not only allowed, but is also a duty, an idea which endures to our days. It is an idea widely followed in disciplines such as genetics, information technology, and robotics.

Bacon described in 1625 his vision of the city of the future in a most striking way: "The end of our foundation is the knowledge of causes, and secret motions of things; and the enlarging of the bounds of human empire, to the effecting of all things possible."[24] The cult of progress was to dominate thought from the nineteenth century right up to the present, and the work which speaks most powerfully of it is the *Esquisse d'un tableau historique des progrès de l'esprit humain* of Condorcet (1793), which links the progress of humanity and society most closely with science and technology.

It was in the 1880s that the idea of progress became closely linked to innovation: that all which is new is progress. Likewise it came to be thought that all which is modern is to be preferred to what is ancient. These two ideas powered the capitalist economy. They justified such policies as built-in obsolescence, and in turn were reinforced by advertising and organized imitation. This served the requirement for the economy to expand through ceaseless production of new products which had to be sold even when they filled no real need for the public.

An idea which is true, that there is no limit to the progress of knowledge and technology, came to be linked to an idea which is false in the long term, that economic development is limitless. This is seen as the wealth of commerce and of states, and to a lesser extent of their populations, which is supposed to grow without limit. In the twentieth century, this led to the consumer society. Citizens must consume ever more goods so that manufacturers and distributers may grow their profits continuously. But when this mechanism breaks down, there is overproduction and waste.

A Mercantile and Utilitarian View of the World

Commercial activities grew steadily from the sixteenth century through trade linked to the discovery of the New World; but it was in the nineteenth century that a purely mercantile and utilitarian vision of the world became common. This was linked to the development of production technology and capitalism. Nature was henceforth taken to be a reserve of resources to be exploited, and the "king of creation" became the "broker of the planet" in the words of the philosopher Antoine-Auguste Cournot.[25] This finally buried the romantic attachment to nature which certain writers and artists had adopted in the seventeenth century as a poor substitute for the spiritual link found in Christianity.

So technology was developed to extract natural resources and improve rates of production in both industry and agriculture. Moreover, commerce flourished through the development of sales and marketing, all of which led to capitalism raising the economic standard of life in Western societies, while at the same time their spiritual life declined. This new system changed people's way of thinking and forced them into a new way of life which attached modern man ever more firmly to material reality, attaching him to "this world" and weakening in him that attachment to God which marks all spiritual life.

Societies of low economic development generally are more open to the spiritual side of life. The poverty, insecurity, misery, and discomfort in which they live make them feel mankind's ontological weakness, dependence, and vulnerability. So hope in a better world grows naturally in their hearts which embrace the spiritual. However, those who live in wealth and comfort, sheltered from difficulties and suffering get a false idea of their independence and strength. Thinking themselves fulfilled and happy, they come to see spiritual life as superfluous and useless, unless they find in it a pleasant pastime for their hours of leisure. We see this in the current fashion for meditation, borrowed from far-eastern spirituality.

The citizens of modern Western societies have materialism stamped on their minds and their way of life. They imbibed it from the enlightenment of the eighteenth century and the atheist philosophers of the nineteenth and early twentieth centuries, Nietzsche, Feuerbach, Marx, and Freud, each making his unique contribution. This materialism took the form of gaining wealth for part of the population and of consumerism for most of it. For modern man, these two activities are his permanent aims and way of life. Deep in his mind is the idea that happiness comes not just from a life sheltered from material need, but also from indulging material desires. It is often said that in traditional religious societies, a man is valued for what he is, but in modern materialistic societies, he is valued solely by what he has.

The capitalist and the bourgeois are marked by the desire of acquiring wealth for its own sake, far beyond their true needs, and measuring their own value by the size of their fortune. As for the modern consumer, he frantically seeks to consume to satisfy artificial wants, desires, and whims which are way beyond his real needs. He has a taste for luxury and is systematically wasteful. All these habits encourage the exploitation of nature, for some a source of riches, and for the rest, a series of objects to be consumed.

Fossil fuels, like coal and oil, and the electrical energy which comes from them have all become great sources of profit. The citizens need these things for heating their homes, filling up their vehicles, and many other things. More surprisingly, even things which used to be taken to be necessities of life, natural blessings common to all such as water and public spaces, which once were freely available and accessible to all, have been taken over by enterprises which exploit them for profit. The beings of nature thus become appropriated for commercial gain. The genetic modification of various edible plants aims at producing patentable seeds which require the use of certain crop protection products which hooks the farmers to their use. In America there are even businesses which have patented certain genetically modified animals and even modified human genes. For man, this is an extension of the age-old process of profiting from people's sickness and their desire for health.

The rise of intensive farming, of the industry and commerce linked to them and of the consumer society leads to tremendous exploitation of natural resources. This is guided by no spiritual principle or ethical norm as to the nature and quantity of the resources extracted nor yet as to the means of extraction and the damage this will do to nature and to man. These activities are controlled by powerful international groups who owe no obedience to the laws and rules of individual states.

This capitalist system of exploiting and commercializing nature has imprinted its special mindset on those who run it. The same mindset has spread to the whole population of modern societies. In the late nineteenth and early twentieth centuries this was unique to Western societies, but it has now spread to the whole world.

As Max Weber showed, capitalism cannot be reduced to an objective system for the production, accumulation, and distribution of wealth. It is also a mentality. In his famous work *The Protestant Ethic and the Spirit of Capitalism,*[26] he shows how capitalism is based on psychological, ethical, and religious factors linked partly to a rational and bourgeois mind; but it is also and especially linked to the most secular protestant form of Christianity which sees in riches a sign of Divine election.

Yet there are further, more general, spiritual factors which are deeper springs of this mentality. These are those passions which have conditions most favorable for their growth in the modern world.

THE AGGRAVATION OF CERTAIN PASSIONS

Egotism

As we have seen, St Maximos the Confessor sees the appearance and growth of passions as a direct consequence of ancestral sin. Man turned away from God and became attached simply to the perceptible appearance of creatures insofar as this satisfied his sensual pleasure.[27] Man no longer related to the beings of nature in Eucharist and contemplation, but desired to possess them and exploit them for his own pleasure. This is why St Maximos saw *philautia,* or self-love, as the key to this decline and considered it to be the mother of all other passions.

Self-love encloses man within himself and destroys his link with God. It also destroys harmonious relations with his fellows. As St Maximos says, it divides man's single nature into a multitude of antagonistic parts. Finally, it destroys nature itself, since man no longer cares to protect and safeguard it, but thinks only of exploiting it for his own pleasure and consuming its products. For sure, modern society did not invent egotism but it made it worse through the individualism which arose in the Renaissance and with its way of life. Thus our lives in Western civilization have become less and less communal and less cohesive.

The Patriarch of Serbia, Paul, writes of the negative effects of modern man's egotism on nature and on humanity itself:

> Man's egotism and his egocentricity make the human race endanger and spoil nature itself, in which we were born and where we live. Just as man lives and breathes in love, so all creatures and all the forces of nature need compassion, love and goodness. The water we drink, the air we breathe, the flowers and trees of the fields, the fish in the sea, the wild beasts in the mountains and our domestic animals, all seek mercy, love and goodness. If it happens that we mistreat one of these elements, or if we misuse it, poison it or pollute it, then this natural element becomes estranged, it disintegrates, falls apart and takes revenge on the one who abused it. Thus the order of things ordained by God is overthrown: water loses its taste, the earth and the crops it yields are contaminated and contaminate those who consume them, men and other creatures. The climate changes; the ice melts at the North Pole; the natural order of the seasons disappears; the rising temperature prepares—may God save us—the earthly globe to be consumed one day by fire.
>
> Moreover, man today controls the outer environment through his technology and so endangers the living space of many other creatures. He no longer devotes himself to the limitless domain of the spirit and its mastery, something which threatens no one and which grants their fullness to all things, opening horizons of growth and perfection beyond telling. Instead, man turns to nature which is limited and passing, and so becomes handicapped and limited himself.[28]

According to St Maximos the Confessor, self-love is closely linked to the body, since it is by means of the body, and often for its sake, that man begins his relationships with the beings of nature.

Science, in spite of its abstract nature, has been set up as a means of knowing the world purely through what is perceptible. Classically, it is defined as "The knowledge of phenomena and their laws." Etymologically, phenomena are those things which appear to the senses whether naked or aided by instruments (from *phanein* meaning to appear).

Technology is set up as a way of exploiting the beings of nature for their utility or for profit. It is classically defined as "A set of procedures put to work to obtain a result which is thought useful."

However, it is above all the modern economy, developed by using technologies based on science, which has amplified the ill effects of human passions.

Greed

In the first place comes greed. It is the attachment to material goods and the wealth they can provide (which the Greek Fathers called *philargyria*) and the desire to acquire and possess more and more (which the Greek Fathers called *pleonexia*). Since greed has become the mainspring of economic activity, the exploitation of nature has grown to hitherto unprecedented levels, far beyond the true needs of mankind. Natural resources are no longer extracted and processed in amounts sufficient to meet the true needs of mankind as they emerge and to maintain life. They are exploited *a priori* and without limit solely in the search for profit and growth.

Farmers and industrialists are driven by greed to seek the greatest yield at the lowest cost. Intensive agriculture is pursued with no thought for the degradation and exhaustion of the soil, and industrial production with no care for the exhaustion of natural resources and the ruin of the environment. The prophet Isaiah had a premonition of this destruction of nature by the passion of greed (Isa 5:9–12). St John Chrysostom commented on this passage which predicts the reduction of natural resources and the desertification of various regions which push whole populations into exile:

> "Of a truth many houses shall be desolate, even great and fair, without inhabitant." (Isa 5:9). Behold the passion of acquisition. When it brings in

> new riches what came before is neglected. Isaiah shows this when he says that by building splendid houses and acquiring the goods of others you lose your own. Those houses will stay standing, but with no inhabitant. They will most plainly accuse those pillagers, for their solitude itself, so striking and prolonged, will be a monument to their owners' sin. "Yea, ten acres of vineyard shall yield one bath, and the seed of an homer shall yield an ephah." (Isa 5:10). After the desolation of the city, he describes the desolation of the countryside so as more strongly to impress his hearers. He proclaims that the houses will be bereft of inhabitants and the land of its productive strength. In the beginning, as punishment for Adam's sin, it brought forth thorns and thistles. Then, through the sin of Cain, it yielded fruit more sparingly, less than the measure of its cultivation and its remaining natural fertility. Moreover, there are many other cases where the earth can be seen as chastised for the crimes of men.

What follows could be thought of as a prophecy of industrial society where men work day and night so much as to lose the sense of night and day. Having no regard for nature or its Creator, they fall ill without knowing it, and rush to their destruction on a road which leads to the lack of the most basic necessities:

> "They regard not the work of the LORD, neither consider the operation of his hands." (Isa 5:12). [The prophet] understands by this [...] the spectacle of nature. How could they contemplate it if they turn day into night and at night are like corpses? How could they see the sunrise, the dazzling beauty of the sky and all the stars which shine at eventide? How could they perceive the order and hierarchy which rules the whole creation when they have lost both outward and inner vision? They have committed a great crime by going through life blind to the wonders which God has created, and spending their time in darkness. [...] "My people are gone into captivity, because they have no knowledge of the Lord." (Isa 5:13). He speaks of the future as though it were the past and warns of the punishment of this crime. [...] But since they had become so insensitive that when punished they felt it not, and when sick, they knew it not, he added the threat of bodily chastisement: "Therefore my people are gone into captivity, because they

have no knowledge: and their honourable men are famished, and their multitude dried up with thirst."[29]

It is not just the producers who are to blame. Greed has made merchants and consumers careless about the limits to natural resources and the way they are exploited. Comfort and value for money have become the main drivers of consumption for the average consumer.

Other passions present in the capitalist system are also to blame. It has competition at its heart which works through the passions of domination, covetousness, jealousy, rivalry, and aggression. Man is used simply as a tool with no regard for his means of existence or his health. This brings out passions contrary to the virtue of love for one's neighbor which Christianity considers to be next in importance to love of God.

The absence of care for creatures, treated simply as objects to be exploited for profit or consumption, bears witness to this lack of love for God. So does a lack of care for our neighbor. This is closely linked to ignorance of God which St Maximos, Evagrius Ponticus, and other Fathers saw as the root of sin and passionate habits from which all else flows.

The words of the prophet Hosea come to mind:

> Hear the word of the Lord, you children of Israel, for the Lord has a judgment for the inhabitants of the land: there is no truth or mercy, or knowledge of God in the land. Cursing and lying, murder and theft and adultery gushed forth in the land, and blood is mingled with blood. Therefore the land shall mourn and be diminished with the things that dwell in it: the wild beasts of the field, the reptiles of the earth, and the birds of the sky, and the fish of the sea shall come to an end.
>
> (Hos 4:1–3)

Covetousness

It is easy to see that the members of modern societies are becoming more and more covetous. They want to possess more and more of better goods and to have what is most up to date in every domain. This covetousness is aroused by producers and merchants who need a ready market for their products and stock which have been created, as we have seen, *a priori* with no thought for mankind's real needs. To this end they use all the sales and advertising techniques developed in the twentieth century, and the force of fashion.

In the economically developed societies of modern times, real needs are swamped by artificial wants, which are simply desires aroused by beguilement. They spread through the force of imitation: the desire to have and to be as the rest of society. At their root, they assuage the passions of consumers to have yet more, something better and something new for their material pleasure. Although advertising is found everywhere, even in the sphere of culture, its main thrust is nonetheless in the material domain, especially in what procures bodily comfort and pleasure. It is easy to see how almost all advertising, in billboards, newsprint, or video is for food, clothing, cosmetics, and all which concerns man's outer appearance. It can also be seen that almost all advertising seeks to excite two basic passions of fallen man and to put them to work: gluttony (sometimes called gourmandize) and sexual lust. The first is stripped of guilt and perversely set up as a virtue. The second gives rise to a profusion of naked bodies in lascivious or provocative poses, giving a sexual connotation to what is being sold.

Covetousness arouses other passions, especially pride: the desire to have more than others, to set oneself apart and to be superior by what one possesses; and vanity: the wish to shine through one's possessions, to appear better and more brilliant and so to arouse the envy of others. Permanent comparison of oneself to others leads to judgment; aggression to compete with and get the better of others; and sadness when one fails to gain what one desires, for advertising skillfully arouses feelings of dissatisfaction and frustration, and of disenchantment even when one's desire is obtained.

The covetousness of modern consumers corresponds to a perversion of both need and desire by submitting both to the passions. Need should be confined to what is necessary for existence, whilst desire should be directed toward the spiritual goal for which it was intended.[30]

Covetousness can never bring satisfaction in the material realm since it is forever fanned by novelties and the goods of others who may own more. It substitutes the limitations of the material world for the infinite spaces of the spiritual world, where the Infinite Himself may be found, the only One Who can satisfy man's endless desire.[31]

To conclude, it can be seen that it is the economic side of the modern world which has become the most important. So it has become a world where the exaggerated greed of the producers and merchants feeds on the exaggerated covetousness of its citizens, the consumers, and vice versa; and it is unable to break free of this vicious circle without recovering those virtues which its passions have destroyed.

Chapter 4

Restoring the Relationship of Man with Nature

POLITICAL AND SOCIAL SOLUTIONS

Social, Political, and Economic Remedies

This book is mainly concerned with the spiritual causes of ecological problems and with the spiritual remedies which can be applied to them. However, as we have already seen, the ecological crisis of our time is strongly bound up with our political and economic systems. So in the short term, it is urgent to remedy it by national and international regulation.

Common sense shows what actions need to be taken. They have already been suggested by various bodies and are summarized below:

1) Reduce the use of artificial fertilizers and pesticides in agriculture, and especially reduce the production of toxic waste by industry. This requires the common action of every state. International agreements are required, because the industries involved are often more powerful than individual states. Whatever is agreed should be enforced by the law.
2) Natural resources, vegetation, and animals at risk of exhaustion, depletion, or extinction should be protected.
3) The development of renewable energy should be encouraged. The wind, the rivers, the tides, and the sun's energy should all be harnessed, so as to bring about an energy transition which replaces, bit by bit, the energies which exhaust the earth or pollute the planet.

4) Develop the repair and recycling of goods, so as to stop the waste and built-in obsolescence linked to the consumer society.
5) Promote the consumption of natural organic foods, cultivated without artificial fertilizer, pesticides, or genetic modification, so that farmers are encouraged to grow them and retailers to sell them.
6) Abandon the religion of endless progress and strive to decrease all which exhausts, damages, or destroys nature.
7) Both states and individuals should accept the price of a more modest life.

Christian Support for Political Action in Favor of Ecology

Christians should be at the forefront of support for measures executed by the authorities which need the support of their citizens. However, political movements aimed at protecting nature often mix in other aims which a Christian cannot support, and this complicates matters. In several European countries, the political movements aimed at supporting ecology and the protection of nature often support, or prioritize, the development of a society incompatible with Christianity, and even with ecology itself: abortion, euthanasia, same-sex marriage, and, for same-sex couples, artificial procreation or the adoption of children.[1]

So Christians can only exercise their votes in favor of ecology in certain cases; but they can always speak out in public when they have the opportunity. This is especially the case for the official representatives of the Churches. They are still viewed as having some moral authority, and all the local Orthodox Churches have expressed their views on this subject many times, through synodal documents and the speeches and publications of their Primates. For example, as mentioned in the introduction, the Patriarch of Constantinople, Bartholomew, has been involved in ecological questions[2] for many years, as was his predecessor, Dimitrios.[3] The Russian Church has also made itself heard through various publications and declarations, especially in 2007[4] and 2013.[5]

In practice, Christians should set a good example by acting in ways which will help to preserve nature. They should prefer renewable energy and natural products whilst avoiding overconsumption and waste.

In several countries Orthodox monasteries show the way through the produce of organic farming and craft work, the propagation of their methods, and the dissemination of the spiritual foundation on which they rest. In France, the monastery of Solan is a good example of this, praised in many articles, publications, and television documentaries.[6]

THE SPIRITUAL FOUNDATIONS AND METHODS FOR RESTORING CREATION

Whatever the value of these social initiatives and ecological gestures, they can only provide partial and provisional solutions. It is clear that the ecological crisis has deep spiritual roots and can only be completely solved by equally deep spiritual remedies which address its root causes.

The Restoration of Man by Christ

Christianity teaches that through his ancestral sin man was enslaved to the power of sin, of the devil, of suffering, corruption, and death. Only Christ, the incarnate Word, was able to restore him. All the efforts on an ethical level of the prophets failed before the superhuman nature of the task.[7] For, as the Fathers say, it required a doctor and surgeon whose skill was equal to the magnitude of these sicknesses and sores.[8] It was Christ, became man with two natures, divine and human, Who was able through His Divine power to raise up, heal, free, and restore in Himself that fallen human nature which He assumed in Himself in all save sin.

The Fathers often compare the salvation brought by Christ to the restoration of the life of paradise. Indeed Christ Himself is called the second or new Adam by St Paul (cf. 1 Col 15:45) and the Fathers who follow him. But does this restoration of the life of paradise apply also to the whole of created nature?

It is clear that many patristic commentaries speak almost exclusively of the restoration of man. The Word became flesh and was incarnate in human nature with a man's soul and body. So the whole course of salvation and its fulfillment in deification are centered on man. Nonetheless, both in Scripture and in the Fathers, there are passages which indicate that the saving and deifying work of Christ embraces, in a certain way and form, the whole of creation.

For example, St Paul uses an all-embracing formula when he writes: "For it pleased the Father that in him should all fulness dwell; And, having made peace through the blood of his cross, 'by him to reconcile all things unto Himself, by Him,' I say, 'whether things on earth or things in heaven'" (Col 1:19–20). Here, peace is not simply the end of war between the nations, or between the chosen people and the gentiles. It is the abolition of conflict, of tension, of contradiction, of discord and lack of harmony between all the beings of creation. This is shown by the phrase "all things" and the reference to both heaven and earth. This is indeed peace, for sin had brought in a rupture and a conflict between man and God and between man and creatures. The disorder in nature caused by the sins and passions of men also takes the form of a conflict between the forces of good and evil. The first aim to preserve the original order of nature, whilst the second seek to destroy it, even down to the level of microbiology and nanophysics.

The peace which Christ brings to nature, to men, to animals, and to plants is described in the prophecy of Isaiah:

> There shall come forth a rod from the root of Jesse, and a flower shall grow out of this root. The Spirit of the God shall rest upon Him, the Spirit of wisdom and understanding, the Spirit of counsel and might, the Spirit of knowledge and godliness. The Spirit of the fear of God shall fill Him. He shall not judge by reputation nor convict by common talk. But He will judge the cause of the humble, and reprove the humble of the earth. He shall strike the earth with the word of His mouth, and with the breath of His lips He shall slay the ungodly. He shall gird His loins with righteousness and cover His sides with truth. The wolf shall feed with the lamb, the leopard shall lie down with the young goat, and the calf, the bull, and the lion shall feed together; and a little child shall lead them. The cow and the bear shall graze together, and their young ones shall lie down together. The lion and the ox shall eat straw together. The nursing child shall play by the hole of asps, and the weaned child shall put his hand in the den of asps. They shall not hurt nor be able to destroy anyone on My holy mountain, for the whole world shall be filled with the knowledge of the Lord, as much as water cover the seas. (Isa 11:1–9)
>
> For ye shall go forth with gladness and shall be taught with joy, for the mountains and hills shall exult to receive you with joy; and all the trees of the field shall applaud with their branches. Instead of the broom-tree

> shall come up the cypress, and instead of nettle shall come up the myrtle; and the Lord shall be for a name and for an everlasting sign, and He shall not fail. (Isa 55:12–15)

At the heart of the Liturgy is the prayer of the anaphora, addressed to the Father, which recalls the words of Christ "Who, when He had come and fulfilled all the dispensation for us, on the night in which He was given up, or rather gave Himself up for the life of the world ..."[9] Christ sacrifices himself "for us men and for our salvation,"[10] as the creed puts it, but the effects of his sacrifice extend beyond us over the whole world.

St Irenaeus emphasizes that by his incarnation, the Word of God enters His own realm where He was already present and over which He has reigned since He created it. By His coming He recapitulates "all things":

> For the Author of the world is in truth the Word of God. He is our Lord: in the last times He Himself was made man, yet He was already in the world (John 1:10). Invisibly He sustained all creation (Wis 1:7) and was everywhere present as the Word of God, governing and arranging all things. This is why "He came" visibly "unto his own" (John 1:11), "was made flesh" (John 1:14) and was hung upon the wood (Acts 5:30; Acts 10:39; Gal 3:13; Deut 27:22–23) that he might gather together in one all things (Eph 1:10) [...]. For He it is, as Word of God and true man, into Whose hand the Father has given all things. He orders the invisible beings spiritually, giving them intelligible laws so that each should remain in his station. Over visible beings and men he reigns manifestly, bringing to all the just judgement that each deserves.[11]

A contemporary saint, Porphyrios of Kapsokalyvia, considers that Christ united in Himself, and in the Church, which is His body, not just man, but all the beings of creation:

> Christ reunited the body of the Church with heaven and earth, with the angels and men, with the animals and birds and each little wildflower and tiny insect. It is thus that the Church has become the fulness of him that filleth all in all (Eph 1:23): Christ. That is the mystery of the Church.[12]

However, to unite something to oneself or within oneself does not mean to become identified with it. It would be quite wrong, and even heretical, to go on to say that Christ has hypostasized the whole universe.[13] Those grave distortions inherent in the theologies of "the cosmic Christ"[14] are unacceptable. They end by confusing Christ with the universe and the universe with Christ, an idea which is not just panentheist but pantheist.

It is true that St Maximos the Confessor speaks of a triple incarnation of Christ: in the *logoi* of creation, in the words of Scripture and in human nature,[15] but he sees them in a hierarchy. The first two, which signify a presence, are called incarnations metaphorically and precede the Incarnation in the flesh where the divine Word takes on exclusively human nature.

Man's Necessary Collaboration

The salvation accomplished by Christ concerns man first of all, and through him extends to all creation since he recapitulates all things in himself and unites them together and to God.[16] Yet this salvation is offered as a pure potential for man and for creation.

The Word gives man once more the ability to fulfill the divine plan, and it is up to him to become, in Christ, the mediator between God and His creatures. In the *Ambiguum 7*, St Maximos envisages that the Creator of all might be proven to be One, and through humanity might come to reside in all beings in a manner appropriate to each, so that the many, though separated from each other in nature, might be drawn together into a unity as they converge around the one human nature. When this happens, God will be all in all, encompassing all things and making them subsist in Himself.[17]

Man can only be a mediator when he is united to Christ, and receives personally and truly the grace which Christ won for humanity for this very purpose. In other books[18] we have shown how this is accomplished by union with the Church. By baptism a person is joined to the body of Christ, and through the various sacraments receives the grace of God. This grace is then assimilated through the ascetic life. This ascetic life, writ large, is the life in Christ which is lived through the practice of His precepts.

There are two sides to the path of Christ's commandments. Firstly, it cleanses man's nature from the passions of sin which have stained him since the fall. Secondly, it cultivates the opposing virtues. The passions, as we have seen, are linked to various negative attachments to oneself and to the world. The virtues attract man to God in various ways, and through Him link man to his fellows and to other creatures in love. To rediscover those normal relations he once had with nature, man must follow the path opposite to the one which brought discord with creatures and damaged his very self.

However, he can only go part way. For the reasons we have set out elsewhere in detail,[19] it is impossible in this world to find again paradise in its fullness, natural, material, and physical:

1) The "old man" does not immediately change into the "new man." It is a slow and difficult path of growth (cf. Matt 7:14; 11:2), and those who take it often fall and stumble so that progress can be patchy and uncertain (cf. 1 John 1:8–10; Rom 3:10–12).
2) Many men deliberately set their will against the salvation offered by Christ and persevere in evil. Since sin persists in the world, its consequences continue to affect both human nature and the whole cosmos. Christ did indeed set aside the law of sin and crush the Devil's tyranny. He removed the spiritual sting of death, but he did not eliminate sin or the works of the demons. He allowed the consequences of sin to remain so as to leave free their cause: man's free will.[20]

Though it is possible for some—the saints—to reach a level of perfection and to bring harmony to their surroundings, this is mainly on a spiritual plane. Their influence over nature is limited. Physically, they are subject to sickness, corruption, and death, though spiritually they may be free of their effects through inner stillness and peace. In general, they cannot prevent the ill effects of the climate, or the strife between different species, or the natural effects of harmful microbes, even though in special cases they may limit them through miracles.

Only at the end of time will all things be restored (cf. Acts 3:21) when God will reveal "new heavens and a new earth, in which righteousness dwells" (2 Pet 3:13). The order and harmony destroyed by sin will be fully restored, and the treasures of grace won by Christ through his redeeming and deifying work will be poured out on all and in every way.

Yet since the Kingdom of Heaven "is already with us" in a certain measure, it is possible to receive an earnest of future perfection already, and by limiting the passions and sins of men, to rediscover something of the order and harmony to come.

The Role of Prayer

Prayer is vital for everything which depends on man's action and for everything which is beyond him. Man's efforts are needed in the struggle against all forms of evil, but are insufficient. The grace of God must complete them. So prayer, which is a plea for this grace, is essential.

From the beginning, the Church has taken care to pray that nature may be clement to men. Since the ancestral sin, this has not always been the case. The elements may show their violence; the climate may be inclement—too hot, too wet, or too cold—and so ruin the harvest; the fertility of the soil, the purity of the air and water may be harmed from natural causes.[21]

In all the liturgical offices of the Orthodox Church (especially Vespers, Matins, and the Liturgy), there is a repeated litany where a prayer is addressed to God "For seasonable weather, abundance of the fruits of the earth, and peaceful times."[22] In the *Book of Needs* (Euchologion), which is the Orthodox Church's prayer book for the clergy, there are many prayers for the fruits of the earth: that they may be brought forth and preserved. There are several offices for the blessing of water, one of the most vital substances for life, for the blessing of wells and for the blessings of vessels or granaries used for storing the essentials of life, that they may be preserved. There is a *blessing of medicinal and culinary herbs* which asks God to preserve their strengthening and healing properties. There are several offices and prayers which concern the climate: *An Office of intercession in times of drought; an Office of intercession in times of inclement weather; Prayer for favorable seasons; Prayer for those who fear lightning and thunder; Prayer in times of bad weather; Prayer for those in danger at sea.* There are other prayers to be read in times of sickness—*An Office of intercession in times of epidemic, an Office of intercession in times a deadly epidemic,* and for animals, *an Office of intercession in times of epizootic disease.* There is also *an Office of intercession in times of earthquakes,* and *Prayers in times of famine.*

These prayers, which seek to remedy the disorders and threats from fallen nature or to protect men from them, can be completed and strengthened by the clergy in special circumstances or for special needs.

The Patriarchate of Constantinople has consecrated the first day of the liturgical year (September 1) to the protection of the environment, and has composed a series of prayers adapted to the occasion which can be inserted into the daily liturgical offices. These prayers are needed by nature itself to assuage its own defects and also by men who can either safeguard it or degrade it.

The Role of Repentance

The salvation of nature can only be accomplished through men whose mentality has been purified. To play their part in this task, as far as is possible, they must change their mentality and way of life and behavior. Repentance (in Greek *metanoia,* which means a change [*meta*] of the state of mind [*nous*]) is of prime importance. Every spiritual undertaking should start with repentance. Indeed it is the first of John the Baptist's exhortations [Matt 3:8; Mark 1:4–5; Luke 3:3–8], and following him, the first of Christ's [Matt 4:17; Mark 1:15]; it should be a constant spur in spiritual life. Man must become aware of his faults: how he has failed himself, his fellow men, and the natural beings which depend on him. He must regret them and firmly resolve to change his ways.

For a Christian, the environment is not a general and ill-defined entity, but is made up of the concrete beings of creation. Like John the Baptist, Christians should encourage all to repent for all their failings toward the creatures which make up the environment. First and foremost, they themselves should repent for all their own failings toward nature: the damage they have caused, their lack of proper care for it, and their failure to behave toward it virtuously and so to set a good example.

Our saintly contemporary from Serbia, the elder Thaddeus, considered that our very thoughts have an enormous influence on our environment. They affect mankind and also animals and plants. Thus we should change our thoughts, and the energy that goes with them if we are to change ourselves and the world around us.

> Divine strength, divine life and divine energy dwell within us. When we come before God at the Last Judgement we will have to account for the way we have used the divine strength, the divine life and the divine energy which we were given and to show whether we have contributed to universal harmony or not.

> Our thoughts do not just act upon ourselves and other reasonable beings, and the animal and vegetable world: they also affect eternity. With our thoughts, we do not just trouble the peace of the earthly globe, we also spread evil throughout the universe. The whole human race reaps the fruits of its thoughts and desires. In the beginning, humanity was drowned in the flood because of its evil thoughts and wicked desires. And once again, we are so buried in evil and unable to free ourselves that such times again draw near for us. The only escape is, with God's help, to transform our inner life with all our heart.
>
> Since the divine energy dwells within us our whole being should be joined to its source, the Lord, so that this energy may be enlivened with divine strength and free us from enslavement to evil. Let us therefore turn to good, so that good may be within us and around us. By concentrating on what is good and turning our thoughts to God we will have inner peace. Through us, peace will radiate around us and help to change things [...] One single soul can, in any situation, have a great influence in this way.[23]

Our thoughts represent our reasonings, our imaginings, our memories, and our sentiments and desires. According to Orthodox spiritual Tradition, they are strongly linked to our passions, of which they are the source, the force, and the expression. We have seen how our transgressions against our neighbor are the expression of almost every passion. So repentance should fundamentally aim to fight against them, to weaken them, and finally to eradicate them.

The Struggle against the Love of Money, Covetousness, and Greed

As we have said, the path to salvation is the opposite of the path leading to the fall, starting from where we are we need to attack first the passions which are most to blame for our present sorry state. These are the crudest of all and are most clearly linked to the evils we wish to overcome.

The first passions to be attacked are *phylargiria* and *pleonexia* which are normally translated into English as covetousness and greed, but which have a broader meaning than the English terms.

What the Fathers call *phylargiria* means the love of money, and also the love of material goods, of riches, and luxury. Its opposite is the voluntary poverty and detachment from material things which are seen as virtues[24] by Christian spirituality.

What the Fathers call *pleonexia* refers to the desire and will to acquire ever more material goods, and to develop one's estate through the increase of wealth. It includes a strong dose of envy, so that in Western Christianity it is often rendered by the Latin word *invidia.* Its opposite also involves detachment from wealth, and furthermore, being content with what is necessary and shunning what is superfluous so as not to envy or desire the surplus of others.

To treat both problems, man must be satisfied with the fulfillment of his basic natural needs, living a simple and modest life marked by sobriety. In economically developed countries at the present time, this would mean "negative growth," and the abandonment of the modern myth of infinite growth and progress. This implies a radical rethinking of our economic system which is entirely based on this myth. It also means a radical change in their way of life for most of the population of wealthy countries.

Asceticism, Temperance, and Sacrifice

What is needed is that everyone should become an ascetic in the strict meaning of the term, which implies effort, renunciation, and privation based on temperance and sacrifice. The Fathers see temperance, in Greek *egkrateia,* as a cardinal virtue.[25] It implies self-control and especially moderation in food and in the use of all those things which procure bodily comfort and pleasure. Sacrifice means giving up some of our goods, some of our wealth, and some of those things which give us a life of ease. It also implies a change in who we are insofar as this depends on what we have. To begin with, this sacrifice is inevitably painful and even sorrowful until a new equilibrium is reached. Still, as Patriarch Bartholomew reminds us in one of his communications,[26] a true Christian life necessarily involves sacrifice. With experience we find that the loss of part of our material goods brings about spiritual gain.

As regards the impact of sacrifice on environmental problems, Patriarch Bartholomew writes:

> In his historical encyclical letter in 1989 [our predecessor, the Oecumenical Patriarch Dimitrios 1st] emphasizes the need for all to acquire an ascetic spirit. [...] This means that we should voluntarily restrict our

consumption of food and natural resources. Each of us is called to distinguish between what we want and what we need. Only by such renunciation and through our willingness sometimes to limit ourselves and to say "No" or "Enough" will we rediscover our true place in the universe. [...] This need for an ascetical spirit can be summarized in one key word: sacrifice. This is exactly what is lacking in our environmental ethics and our ecological action. [...] There will never be any real or concrete changes in the environment if we are not ready for radical sacrifices, difficult and truly generous. If we sacrifice nothing we will gain nothing. It is clear that for both nations and individuals much more is required of the rich than the poor. Yet all are called to sacrifice something for the sake of their fellow citizens. [...] Sacrifice is above all a spiritual rather than an economic matter. When we speak of sacrifice, we speak of an ethical rather than a technological question. [...] We often speak of the environmental crisis; but the true crisis is not in the environment but in the heart of man. [...] For the modern world it is outdated, and even unpopular to speak of sacrifice; but if the idea of sacrifice is unpopular it is mainly because many people have a false idea of what sacrifice means. They imagine that sacrifice means loss or death and see it as something dark and sad. [...] However, if we look at the way sacrifice was seen in the Old Testament, we find that the Hebrews saw its significance in quite another way. For them, sacrifice meant not loss but gain, not death but life. Though sacrifice was costly it did not lead to loss but to fulfilment. It signified a change for the better, not for the worse. Above all, for the Hebrews, sacrifice did not mean to deprive, but simply to give. [...] It had to be spontaneous and voluntary. What is taken from us by force and violence against our will is not a sacrifice. Only what we offer in freedom and love is a true sacrifice. Without love, there is no sacrifice. When we give up something against our will, we suffer loss, but when we offer it willingly, we cannot but gain. [...] Christ proclaimed this strange mystery when he taught "Whosoever will save his life shall lose it," (Mt 10, 39 et 16, 25). When we sacrifice our life and share our riches, we gain life in abundance and enrich the whole world. This is the experience of humanity throughout the ages: *kenosis* means *plerosis*: a voluntary emptying leads to fulfilment. We should apply this in our actions to save the environment. There can be no salvation for the world or hope of a better future without the dimension of sacrifice which we lack. Without a costly and determined sacrifice we can never act as the priests of creation to reverse the spiral of environmental destruction.

The path which lies before us [...] is described most strikingly in the ceremony of the Great Blessing of the Waters, celebrated by the Orthodox Church on 6th January, the Feast of the Theophany, when we commemorate the Baptism of Christ in the River Jordan. After a doxology which embraces the whole cosmos comes the culmination of the ceremony of blessing: the celebrant takes the Cross, and plunges it into a vessel full of water (if the service takes place in the church) or into the sea or a river if it takes place outdoors.

The Cross is the symbol which guides us in the supreme sacrifice to which we are called. It sanctifies the waters, and through them, transforms the whole world. Who can forget the imposing symbol of the Cross in the splendid mosaic of the Basilica of St. Apollonarius in Classe? Whilst celebrating the Divine Liturgy in Ravenna our gaze was fixed on the Cross placed at the center of our heavenly vision, in the midst of the natural beauty which surrounded it and at the center of our celebration of heaven on earth.

Such is the model which should guide our efforts on behalf of the environment. This is the foundation of all the ethics of the environment. The Cross must be plunged into the waters, the Cross must be at the center of our vision. Without the Cross, without sacrifice, there can be no blessing or transfiguration of the cosmos.[27]

Sacrifice may seem painful, and indeed it is compared to the way of life in developed economies with habits going back a century. The idea of economic contraction may seem difficult from our pampered point of view, or even impossible in the light of the faith in progress instilled in our minds. But for thousands of years, traditional societies have given examples of a modest lifestyle on the material plane leading to the gain of spiritual wealth. This is entirely compatible with happiness and contentment on a higher level and is its prerequisite.

In Christianity itself, turning away from desires and pleasures of the flesh, in the broadest sense, aims to allow spiritual desire to grow, bringing greater spiritual joy.

For sure, sobriety is a remedy for the insatiability aroused by the modern world to serve its idol of limitless growth and its illusion that true happiness comes from the unbridled satisfaction of material desires. For this pursuit of material goods shows its true colors in the dissatisfaction, frustration, and depression of modern man, far greater than anything known in societies of the past.

Fasting as a School of Sobriety

In the Calendar of the Orthodox Church, more than half the days of the year are days of fasting: certain days of the week and days of the annual fasts. This serves as good training in sobriety. Fasting has various aims which we have analyzed elsewhere.[28] Six of them are important for the matter in hand:

1) Fasting helps the one who practices it to be more temperate, and better to master his instincts impulsions and desires linked to the body.
2) Fasting helps him to be more restrained in his desires and even in his needs, since it involves both a reduction of the quantity consumed and in the kind of food eaten: no animal products. The Fathers see this as a reflection of paradise, since there, as we have seen, man ate no flesh.[29] They also see it as a foretaste of the future Heavenly Kingdom where man will have no need of material food since his body will be renewed in a new immaterial form of being. The habit of an Orthodox monk is known as the "angelic habit." This signifies that the monastic life is seen as a mirror of angelic life, and monks stick to a vegetarian regime in their aim to live the life of paradise in this fallen world.
3) During fasting periods there are not only restrictions on food, but also the abandonment of luxury and all that is superfluous.
4) Fasting helps us to lay aside fleshly pleasure and to cease to see the world around us as an object of pleasure, but instead to rise to a more spiritual vision of the world.
5) By refocusing his life onto spiritual things, man acquires a taste for true values. He rediscovers the virtue and joy of living more soberly in the world, and so becoming richer in his relations with God, his neighbor, and nature.

6) Finally, fasting is linked to charity. As we have seen, the ecological crisis has evil effects on both nature and man. Many are condemned to exile, need, poverty, misery, and sickness through climate change, exhaustion of resources, and pollution. If wealthy people restrain their consumption, more can be shared with the disfavored, imparting the surfeit of the first to fill the need of the second. This applies to the present. Yet by limiting our own consumption of nature's goods here and now, we also leave more for generations still to come, who will certainly need them; but without our present restraint they may be exhausted by the time those generations are born.

When the Church Fathers speak of fasting, they link it to almsgiving, or sharing one's goods with others, and to the love of our neighbor. St John Chrysostom writes: "Almsgiving gives strength to fasting. If you fast without almsgiving God will not accept your fast."[30] He adds: "Do not see fasting simply as abstention from food; that would be an insult. If you fast truly, show it through your works. Which works, you may ask me. If you see a poor man, take pity on him."[31] St Gregory Palamas advises the same: "When you fast and restrict your food, do not save the surplus for the morrow. The Lord made us rich by becoming poor, and you, through your voluntary hunger, should feed those who feel hunger unwillingly."[32]

The Struggle with Egotism

This brings us to consider further the struggle with *philargyria* and *pleonexia*. At the root of these two passions, and indeed of all passions, lies egotistical self-love, or *philautia*. This kind of love is the opposite of love of God and neighbor,[33] or true love of one's own good. It is also opposed to the spiritual love of nature. Just as the passions displace the virtues so self-love displaces true love.

Man has no hope of coming to love nature with true respect unless he eradicates this passion, no more than to find true love of God or his neighbor. And since this passion is the mother of all the others, they too must be eradicated in the process. Once more, this means to follow the path opposite to the fall.

As we have shown elsewhere,[34] true love of God and neighbor, of oneself, and of all creatures, is not sentimental. It is a spiritual love which is fixed ontologically, not sentimentally, on its object. It requires ontological rejection of all that opposes it. Every passion is a form of pathological attachment to this world of appearances, as it appears to the despiritualized gaze and desire of those who cannot look beyond it. For the Fathers, love does not come all at once, but grows in man as he is cleansed of his passions. There are broadly two sides to ascetic life: cleansing from the passions and acquisition of virtue. They depend on each other, since the fall of man caused the virtues to be replaced by passions. Thus, according to the Fathers, eliminating the passions leads the virtues to reappear anew.

So it is by cleansing himself from the passions and the self-love in which they reside that man may come truly to love and respect nature, and all the beings it contains.

Coming Anew to the Contemplation of Nature and Seeing God's Presence Therein

The Fathers saw that the cleansing of passions led to the growth of love, which would enable man to contemplate nature truly. He would be able to see the presence of God there through His energies and the *logoi* of His creatures, and to see the relationship of each creature to God. Love and contemplations reinforce each other. By loving creation, man perceives God, and seeing His presence in creatures he loves them even more. Dostoyevsky writes of this:

> Love all creation, as a whole and in its elements: each leaf, each ray of light, the animals and the plants. By loving all things you will understand the divine mystery within them. Once you have understood, you will grow in knowledge each day, and will finally love the whole world with a universal love.[35]

Laying a Strong Foundation for the Respect of Creation

This is the starting point for a true respect of creation. The respect of nature cannot truly be based on a simple legal or moral code. For such codes, in themselves, are relative not absolute.[36] They must be based on the faith that it is God Who gives worth to nature since He is its creator. He protects it with His Providence insofar as man's liberty, which God respects, allows. He is also its end through the *logoi* which it bears within. Nature can only be truly respected when the sacred and transcendent dimension of its relation to God is recognized.

Loving Creation

Christians are used to speaking of love of God and one's neighbor, but not of the love for creatures. However, St Nicholas Velimirovich reminds us that such love is an essential part of Christian charity. In his short work, entitled *The Pyramid of Paradise*, analogous to *The Ladder of Divine Ascent* by St John Climacus, he writes:

> The fifth level of the pyramid of paradise is built from charity. Every stone of this level represents an act of mercy, to one's soul or to men, to animals or to any creature of God. And this level shines out entirely in heavenly blue as though it were a sapphire.[37]

Another saint of our day, Father Amphilochios (Makris) of Patmos, saw in the love of creatures a commandment unwritten maybe, yet given by God.[38]

With cleansing of the passions comes spiritual love and contemplation which lead to a true love of one's neighbor and that true love of creatures and creation which alone can preserve them. This spiritual love of creatures is not passionate and carnal. It is not based on appearances aroused by the passions. Nor is it sentimental or idolatrous. It is not founded on seeing creatures as absolutes to be venerated in place of the Creator (cf. Rom 1:25). The creatures are not just loved for themselves but because of the relationship with God which gives them their worth.

The Fathers show this love of creatures firstly in the compassion they have for those of them who suffer. To the question: "What is a merciful heart?" St Isaac the Syrian replies:

> It is the heart's burning for the sake of the entire creation, for men, for birds, for animals, for demons, and for every created thing; and by the recollection of them the eyes of a merciful man pour forth abundant tears. From the strong and vehement mercy which grips his heart and

> from his great compassion, his heart is humbled and he cannot bear to hear or to see any injury or slight sorrow in creation. For this cause he offers up tearful prayer continually even for irrational beasts, for the enemies of truth and for those who harm him, that they may be protected and receive mercy. And in like manner, he prays even for the family of reptiles because of the great compassion that burns without measure in his heart in the likeness of God.[39]

A contemporary spiritual teacher, Elder Thaddeus from Serbia writes:

> When man is joined to the Lord, this means that he is totally united with Him: his soul is then at peace and bathed in delight. A soul in this state is ever ready to weep over the destiny of her fellow … As soon as she sees suffering in the animal or vegetable world, or the world of men, as soon as she sees that all are suffering, then straightway her tears start to flow. At every moment such a soul is able to weep for all of us. This shows that such a soul is touched by the grace of God, and that these are tears of joy granted by the Lord.[40]

Many such examples of this compassion can be found in the lives of the saints. St Silouan, who dwelt on Mt Athos at the beginning of the twentieth-century, records in his diary the following incidents:

> Once I needlessly killed a fly. The poor thing crawled on the ground hurt and mangled, and for three whole days I wept over my cruelty to a living creature, and to this day the incident remains in my memory.
>
> Somehow it happened that some bats bred on the balcony of the storeroom where I was, and I poured boiling water over them, and once again I shed many tears on this account, and since then I have never harmed any living creature.
>
> One day, going from the Monastery to Old Russikon-on-the-Hill, I saw a dead snake on my path which had been chopped into pieces, and each piece writhed convulsively, and I was filled with pity for every living creature, every suffering thing in creation, and I wept bitterly before God.

He goes on to say that such compassion for the beings of nature is not a natural sentiment, but a fruit of the grace of God:

> The Spirit of God teaches the soul to love every living thing so that she would have no harm come to even a green leaf on a tree, or trample underfoot a flower of the field. Thus the Spirit of God teaches love towards all, and the soul feels compassion for every being.[41]

Love of Nature and Love of Neighbor

The present ecological crisis shows how love of nature and love of neighbor are closely intertwined. There are many ill effects from modern forms of production, be they intensive agriculture with artificial fertilizers and pesticides, the food industry which adds chemicals to foodstuffs, or industry in general which adds dangerous chemicals to everyday products. The ground, the air, and the water table are polluted by these activities whose waste damages the ozone layer and assists global warming and the extreme weather which attends it. The seasons are put out of joint with storms, floods, and heatwaves all of which have grave consequences for ordinary people by provoking and aggravating illnesses, causing famines, and displacing whole populations into exile. All this threatens future generations with a nature so exhausted that it cannot meet their basic needs. Since mankind's bodily existence is so closely linked to nature, any damage to nature damages mankind as well, and any destruction of nature destroys men too. Yet every care given to nature is also a benefit to humanity. Since man and nature depend on each other, love of neighbor and love of nature are indissociable. They affect each other; each implies the other and calls it forth.

Christianity highly esteems the value of the human being, seen as created in the image of God. Thus each person has a unique and irreplaceable character. Love of neighbor is linked to love of God and is the second great commandment after love of God. So, in that love of nature contributes to the love of our neighbor, it is essential.

Dimitru Staniloae, a contemporary Romanian theologian, emphasizes that, in this world, nature is a realm where human relations are formed. Thus men may either do each other evil or good through the way they treat nature, negatively or positively:

> By corrupting, sterilizing and poisoning nature man makes his own existence impossible and does the same to his fellows. So nature is not only the condition for a man's existence, but also for human solidarity. Nature appears perfectly clearly as the realm where man can do good or evil to his fellows, either by improving himself, or by corrupting himself ethically and spiritually. Nature sits in the midst of this dialogue of mankind between benevolence and destruction which underlies the existence of each man and of the whole of humanity.[42]

In the Orthodox Church ecology is sometimes accused of trying to take the place of theology and of developing concerns which draw man away from spiritual life. But as Nicolas Berdiaev wrote, whenever my neighbor suffers in a material way it becomes a spiritual problem. One may add that it is the same when any of God's creatures is ill-used.

The lives and teachings of Orthodox spiritual guides show a certain vision of the solidarity between man and nature. Both are linked to God in their origins and in the care shown them by Divine Providence. "How can you not feel that you are one with all creatures?"[43] said St Porphyrios.

Love of Nature and Love of God

We have seen how the love of God is the true foundation for love of nature, but it is also true that a pure and innocent love of creatures can lead us to love God. St Porphyrios, a contemporary Greek Orthodox saint, expresses it thus:

> Rejoice over everything which surrounds you. All things teach us of God, all things lead us to God: living and lifeless beings, plants and animals, animals and birds, mountains and seas, the sunset and the starry sky. Through these small loves we come to the great Love which is Christ. The flowers, for example, have a special grace: they teach us with their perfume and their magnificence. They speak to us of the love of God. They spread out their odors and their beauty over the just and the unjust alike.

> To become Christian, one must have the soul of a poet. One must become a poet. Christ does not want coarse souls at his side. Simply by loving, the Christian is a poet. He is part of poetry. It is the poetic souls who make love their own possession, who set it in their heart and embrace it, feeling it deeply.
>
> Learn how to "profit" from moments of beauty. Such moments dispose the soul to pray. They make her delicate, noble and poetic. Rise up in the early morning. Go to gaze on the rising of the Sun, the king, in purple hue above the sea. When beautiful scenery, a small chapel or anything lovely inspires your enthusiasm, do not delay. Go beyond the object itself: for everything of beauty, give glory so as to live with the only true Beauty. All is holy, the sea, swimming in the sea and our food. Be joyful in everything. All things enrich us, everything draws us to the great Love, everything draws us to Christ[44]!

In another passage, St Porphyrios describes how love of God and love of creatures interact and reinforce each other:

> Our love for Christ shows itself in the following way: we raise our inner "I" to Christ and we call on His Name. So when we see nature, the trees, the flowers, the birds, the bees, the sea, the fish, the stars, the moon, the sun and all His other wonderful creatures, we turn in spirit to God. As we glorify Him through them, we come to understand how beautiful are these creatures and to love them. When we have loved them all, then our love rises up to our Creator, and thus, in truth and reality we love Him.[45]

The Rediscovery of a Eucharistic Attitude in Our Relation to Creatures

In the end we must change our attitude to nature, no longer to see it as an object of prey, exploitation, or selfish pleasure, but as a Eucharist. This was the calling of the first man, and through him, of all humanity, but all fell short through sin.

A passage from Clement of Alexandria, written in prophetic style, denounces man's commercial use of animals which do them to death. To the baptized, who rediscover the eucharistic use of earthly goods, he promises the recovery of the spiritual form of their possession which God decreed in the beginning:

> The Lord inviteth us to the bath, to salvation, to illumination as if crying out: I give thee, saith He, the earth, the sea and the sky, my child, and I confer on thee all the animals who are found therein; only, my child, thirst for thy Father, and God will show himself to thee freely. For truth cannot be negotiated. He will grant thee the birds, the fish and the animals which dwell in the world. All this the Father hath created that thou mayst delight in it with thanksgiving. The bastard buyeth these with money: a child of perdition preferring to serve Mammon (cf. Matt 6:24; Luke 16:13); but to thee God giveth thy goods, to thee the true son who lovest his Father. Thou art the son for whom He worketh still (cf. John 5:17); to thou alone He hath made this promise: "The land shall not be sold forever." Indeed, it is not destined for destruction "for the land is Mine" (Lev 25:23), and it is also thine if thou receivest God.[46]

Christian life implies that man's everyday relationship with the beings of nature should be eucharistic. This is normal. It is what is manifest in the community within the Orthodox Church at those liturgical seasons when nature is blessed: the blessing of the waters, rivers, lakes, and the sea at Theophany, the baptism of Christ; the blessing of branches on Palm Sunday, where the branches are borne as witness to our thanksgiving and spiritual joy; and the blessing of fruits at the feast of the Transfiguration. It is manifested too in the countryside when the clergy, with the people in procession, bless the fields, the cattle, and the harvest, not simply seeking their protection and an abundant yield, but also giving thanks for everything. It can be seen daily in family life in the prayers before and after the meal, where the fruits of nature which are eaten are seen as the gifts of God Whose blessing we rightly ask and to Whom we rightly give thanks. And as our personal spiritual life deepens, it too becomes constantly eucharistic.

In a beautiful passage, Clement of Alexandria writes of those who attain to a lofty spiritual life. He calls it "gnostic," meaning having knowledge of God. He says that these people give thanks continually for everything, and thus live their whole lives as a joyful festival:

> We are commanded to revere and honor the Word, we who are convinced by faith that He is our saviour and governor. Through Him we honor and revere the Father, not just on special days as others do, but continually throughout our lives and by every means. Indeed, the chosen people, justified by the commandment says: "Seven times a day do I praise thee" (Ps 118/119, 164). Thus it is not in some special place, nor in a chosen sanctuary, nor simply on feasts and appointed days, but throughout his life that the gnostic honors God, in every place whether alone or with others who share his faith: he confesses his thanks for this knowledge and way of life. The presence of a good man molds the one who chooses his company, improving him continuously through a feeling of respect and reverence. How much more then, does the one who is always in the presence of God through knowledge, life and constant thanksgiving, become all the time better than he was in every way, in his works, words and inclinations? Such is the man convinced that God is everywhere present. He does not believe Him to be enclosed in special places so that he may give himself up to intemperance, thinking to be separated from Him night and day. Leading our whole life like a festival, convinced that God is everywhere present, we offer praise as we till the fields; we sail the seas singing hymns; and we lead our whole life obeying the rules. As for the gnostic, he enjoys closer intimacy with God. He is both serious and joyful in every circumstance: serious because he is turned towards the divine; joyful because he reckons up the good things specific to humanity which God has given us.[47]

The Hope That the World May Be Changed If We Change Ourselves

Some may find the spiritual solutions set out above utopic. Humanity behaves in the mass less and less in a Christian way. It is engaged instead in technological and economic processes which appear irreversible. Yet Christianity has always hoped to change the world by purifying it of sin and finding again the lost paradise and even more. It seeks to bring the world as far as possible to a foretaste of the Kingdom which is first accomplished in the Church. The hope is that the Church may extend over all the world, concretely and not just figuratively, so that the world abides in her and identifies with her.

The goal of Christianity was never to establish the Kingdom of Heaven on earth, for Christ said: "My kingdom is not of this world" (John 18:36). Nor does it try to impose itself and its *ethos* on all people by human means.

In the first centuries, Christians were immersed in a pagan world where all manner of deviant behavior abounded. Yet the Apologists[48] did not stress criticism of what they saw as conflicting with Christian ethics. Instead they took a positive line, emphasizing the superiority of Christian values. The Fathers always stressed the prime importance of example, always reminding their flock that we need to change first our own behavior if we are to change the behavior of others. For an exemplary life carries far more conviction than any sermon. Christianity has always taught that it is not by changing society that men can be changed, but by changing men that society can be changed.

Society is not just a set of structures which regulate men, even if these structures can exert powerful pressures; nor is it the sum of individuals governed by economic and social laws. It is a community of free persons, who together are able to define the form and ethos of the society in which they live.

As Pierre Rahbi says quite rightly that the desired improvement in this world in which we live "starts with ourselves: in each of us, for the world cannot be built simply on external structures but on the power of our own subjectivity. Politics is not just the concern of politicians; it is what we apply to ourselves. It is our personal and civic responsibility to develop our being so that it changes and becomes fulfilled. Every time that a person from the depths of his heart has the desire and determination to effect a profound change, every time he takes it in hand and works to bring it about in his own humanity, respecting the basic laws of life and nature, he brings about a change in society. For we are society, and society is made up of every one of us."[49]

The true apostolic and missionary spirit excludes all kinds of constraint or beguilement and always respects the liberty of man. It is based on the hope of bringing as many people as possible to salvation as Christ intends: "Who desires all men to be saved and to come unto the knowledge of the truth" (1 Tim 2:4). The salvation of a great multitude has wide repercussions. It does not just affect each person and the race of men, but nature too in which they live. For as we have shown in different ways, the state of nature is closely linked to the state of humanity.

The Example of the Saints

The lives of the saints witness to the influence of their example on other men. From their impassibility, gained by mortifying all the passions, is born that inner peace which shines out over men, animals, and plants alike. A great modern saint, St Paisios, who lived in harmony with animals, even the wildest, writes:

> Keeping the commandments allows man once more to draw near to God and put off the coat of skins of the old man. Then God clothes him anew with His grace and man is returned to his original state which he had before the fall. Then he lives in innocence amongst men and without fear amongst the wild animals who sense from afar his innocence and love. They approach him once more and lick him with respect. They recognize him as their master and cease being fierce since their master is peaceful.
>
> O blessed desert, who greatly helps God's creature to be reconciled to his Creator. You change yourself into an earthly paradise and gather the wild animals around the man to whom you have given peace.[50]

Filled with peace and love, the saints show deep compassion for every suffering creature and great respect for every being created by God. Around them the world becomes reconciled, freed from conflict and division, which leads to a harmonious symbiosis between men and all the creatures of nature. Animals, plants, and minerals rediscover the spiritual unity which once they had and will have again.

The positive effects of the saints on their environment and the peace they bring to all beings close at hand which so attracts them come from the radiance of their inner state. It is peaceful because purified from passions and is full of love for all creatures and all things.

A great contemporary spiritual guide from Serbia, elder Thaddeus, taught that our thoughts have an enormous influence on those who surround us, and on the animals and plants in our environment. In his simple teaching, based on experience, our thoughts include our desires and feelings, not just our reasonings:

> A thought has enormous force and power. It exerts its influence on reasonable beings, on animals, on plants and all that exists. If our thoughts

are peaceful and serene, they bring peace to our hearts and all those around us as they radiate out from us.[51]

Our thoughts come to pass. They have great force. So our thoughts should be noble and exalted. For we radiate them, transmitters and receivers of incredibly powerful thoughts. Our thoughts act in an incredible way. Learned men have found that our thoughts act not just on reasonable creatures and animals, but on the world of plants which also have their nervous system.

Our life is in the image of our thoughts. If our thoughts are calm, peaceful, serene and humble then peace dwells in us. It shines out from us and influences the nervous system of each being, whether man or beast or plant.[52]

The perfection of Christian life, as all the Holy Fathers testify, is extreme humility. Extreme humility signifies perfection in human life. Every humble and meek soul is nourished by peaceful and calm thoughts, full of love and goodness, which radiate out to living creatures and inanimate things. Our thoughts represent a huge energy within us which is why our lives are the image of the thoughts which we nourish.

Our thoughts influence not just ourselves but all that surrounds us. If our thoughts are peaceful and calm, they have a good influence on the nervous system of each reasonable creature as well as on animals and plants. The vegetable world feels our thoughts. I have been impressed by the number of investigations which have proved that the vegetable world feels our thoughts and looks to us to treat it with attention and love.[53]

The Witness of Icons

The icons express in their own symbols harmony regained between man, nature, and all its creatures thanks to the mediation of grace-filled men. Nature is always shown in a stylized way in icons. The physical environment—mountains, rivers, and deserts—the plants and animals are all turned toward the image of the saint placed at the center and are lightened by the light which first lightens the saint. All seem to commune in divine grace, each according to its nature. In icons, our world is recognizable in a general sense, but their symbolism goes beyond it. Everything is stylized, the animals and plants have simple forms which are slightly offbeat, whilst the colors of feathers and fur are unusual. This stylization creates a general effect which is both luminous and peaceful. It shows us symbolically a transfigured world, raised to new life. This transfigured world evokes "the new heaven and the new earth" foretold by the prophet Isaiah and the book of Revelation. It makes firm our hope to see our own world transfigured through the synergy of our own efforts and of divine grace.

Notes

INTRODUCTION

1 See R. DARQUES, "Logiques de protection de l'environnement en Grèce: le cas de la péninsule athonite," *Méditerranée*, 105, 2005, p. 73–80.

2 See L. LARCHER, *La Face cachée de l'écologie*, Cerf, Paris, 2004. This idea has influenced Catholic theologians like Matthew Fox with his theory of the "Cosmic Christ" and "Mother Earth" set out mainly in *The Coming of the Cosmic Christ: the Healing of Mother Earth and the Birth of a Global Renaissance*, Harper One, New York, 1988. Orthodox theologians have also been influenced, like P. SHERRARD in *The Rape of Man and Nature: an Enquiry into the Origins and Consequences of Modern Science*, Golgonooza Press, Ipswich, 1987, of M.M. EGGER, *La Terre comme soi-même. Repères pour une ecospiritualité*, Labor et Fides, Genève, 2012. However, these are marginal figures who do not represent the official positions of either the Catholic or Orthodox Churches. Indeed, Fox was forbidden to teach by Cardinal Ratzinger and went on to join the Episcopalian Church. There are other odd views to be found on the fringes of Christianity. There is the ecofeminist movement represented especially by Rosemary Radford Ruether, Elizabeth Johnson, and Sallie McFargue. In their thought the Trinity is feminine, and the Holy Spirit and the Divine Wisdom are seen as feminine principals. The Creation is seen as the body of God. Another such view is process theology which is derived from the mathematician A.N. Whitehead's process philosophy. It was developed by Charles Hartshorne, William Temple, Daniel Day Williams, John B. Cobb Jr., and Schubert Ogden. It casts doubt on God's traditional attributes, considering God to be both masculine and feminine, immanent to the World: a

permanent and endless source of creativity, liberty, and novelty, and of budding and growth. Reality is identified with this process of constant movement. These ideas were adopted by certain Protestant theologians, particularly by the Frenchman André Gounelle.

3 "Environmentalism as Religion," *Commonwealth Club*, September 15, 2003 [Trans. A.A. Torrance].

4 This is stated in most of the documents published by the Churches referred to above, but is very strongly emphasized in the vast study of Michel Maxime EGGER, *La Terre comme soi-même*, Genève, 2012.

HOW IT WAS IN THE BEGINNING: MAN'S ORIGINAL RELATIONSHIP WITH NATURE

1 Cf. BASIL OF CAESAREA, *Homélies sur l'Hexaéméron* [Homilies on the six days of Creation], I; SC 26 bis, Paris, 1968, p. 108.

2 See, for instance, the poetical account of GREGORY OF NYSSA, *La Création de l'homme* [The Creation of man]; PG 44, 132A, SC 6, p. 88–9.

3 See the American historian, LYNN WHITE, "The Historical Roots of Our Ecological Crisis," *Science*, 155, 1967, p. 1203–7. The author is a historian, but this famous article is supported by very little other work and is marred by poor arguments. The Metropolitan of Pergamos, John ZIZIOULAS, places the responsibility on Catholicism and Protestantism ("Orthodoxy and Ecological Problems: a Theological Approach," in D. TATAISOS (ed.), *The Environment and Religious Education*, Editions Militos, 1997, p. 26–30). But two other Orthodox authors, Philip SHERRARD (*The Rape of Man and Nature: an Enquiry into the Origins and Consequences of Modern Science*, Golgonooza Press, Ipswich, 1987; *Christianity: Lineaments of a Sacred Tradition*, Holy Cross Orthodox Press, Boston, 1998) and Michel Maxime EGGER (*La Terre comme soi-même*. Genève, 2012) blame Christianity in general. They were influenced by the religions of the Far East through the perennialism of René Guenon and Frithjof Schuon's theory of the transcendent unity of religions, which tend to promote pantheism and paganism.

4 This tendency can be found in the work of Michel Maxime EGGER cited above, and in articles he has written in support of it. He ceaselessly criticizes the anthropocentrism he sees in most Christian authors and downgrades man's nature and his place amongst the other creatures. This author claims to be Orthodox, but his ideas are strongly influenced by Hinduism and tend toward a kind of pantheist monism. Though he claims that they are panentheist, they are in fact close

to neo-paganism. Jean-Claude POLET criticizes them strongly in the Orthodox publication *Contacts*, vol. LXIV, no. 240, October–December 2012, p. 506–14.

5 *Chandogya Upanishad*, 6, 7, 8.

6 See GREGORY OF NYSSA, *La Création de l'homme* [The Creation of man], II; PG, 44, 132D-133B, SC 6, p. 90–1; JOHN CHRYSOSTOM, *Discours contre ceux qui se scandalisent* [Against those who are scandalized], II, 7: "O man, this universe which is so admirable and harmonious was made by the Lord for thee and thee alone."

7 Cf. *Exposé précis de la foi orthodoxe* [An Exact Exposition of the Orthodox Faith]. 24, (II, 10), SC 535, p. 278–80.

8 *Lettres spirituelles* [Spiritual Letters], no. 62, L'Age de l'Homme, Lausanne, 2005, p. 197.

9 See especially St Maximos the Confessor to whom Lars THUNBERG has dedicated a fine work entitled *Microcosm and Mediator.* See also St JOHN OF DAMASCUS, *Exposé précis de la foi orthodoxe* [An Exact Exposition of the Orthodox Faith], 26, (II, 12), SC 535, p. 300.

10 Cf. St GREGORY OF NYSSA, *Sur l'âme et la résurrection* [On the soul and the resurrection], 12, PG, 46, 28B.

11 *Sur les inscriptions des Psaumes* [On the inscriptions of the Psalms], III, PG, 44, 440C.

12 Cf. St JOHN OF DAMASCUS, *Exposé précis de la foi orthodoxe* [An Exact Exposition of the Orthodox Faith], 26, (II, 12), SC 535, p. 300.

13 *Discour* [Discourses], XXXVIII, 11, SC, 358, Paris, 1990, p. 124–6.

14 See GREGORY OF NYSSA, *La Création de l'homme* [The Creation of man], VIII, PG 44, 144D-148B; JOHN OF DAMASCUS, *Exposé précis de la foi orthodoxe* [An Exact Exposition of the Orthodox Faith]; 26, 38, 39, 41 (II, 12, 24, 25, 27), SC535, p. 298–300, 304–6, 344–6, 349–50, 354–6; NICETAS STETHATOS, *De l'âme* [On the soul], 31–2, 38, SC 81, p. 92–4, 100–102. It is in his freedom that man's superiority mainly lies, for though the animals have some degree of intelligence they have no capacity for self-determination or choice.

15 Cf. CLEMENT OF ALEXANDRIA, *Stomates*, II, 19, GCS II, p. 169; *Protreptique*, X, 98, 4, SC 2, p. 166; ORIGEN, *Homélies sur la Genèse* [Homilies on Genesis], I, 13, SC 7 bis, p. 62; *Contre Celse* [Against Celsus], VI, 63, SC 147, p. 336; ATHANASIOS OF ALEXANDRIA, *Sur l'incarnation du Verbe* [On the incarnation of the Word], III, 3, SC 199, p. 272; BASIL OF CAESAREA, *Sur l'origine de l'homme* [On the origin of man], I, 6–7, SC 160, p. 178–82; 11, p. 194; 17, p. 210; GREGORY OF NYSSA, *La Création de l'homme* [The Creation of man], IV, PG 44, 136BC;

XII, PG 44, 161D; CYRIL OF ALEXANDRIA, *Contre les anthropomorphites* [Against the anthromorphites], PG 76, 1069–72; MAXIMOS THE CONFESSOR, *Mystagogie* [Mystagogy], VI, PG 91, 684CD; *Lettres* [Letters], 6, PG 91, 429B; 23, PG 91, 605D; *Dispute avec Pyrrhus* [Disputation with Pyrrhus], PG 91, 304C, 324CD; JOHN OF DAMASCUS, *Exposé précis de la foi orthodoxe* [An Exact Exposition of the Orthodox Faith], 26 (II, 12), SC 535, p. 300.

16 See BASIL OF CAESAREA, *Sur l'origine de l'homme* [On the origin of man], I, 16–17, SC 160, p. 206–10; 18, p. 214–16; JOHN CHRYSOSTOM, *Sermons sur la Genèse* [Sermons on Genesis], III, SC 433, p. 204; DIADOQUE DE PHOTICE, *Cent chapitres* [A hundred chapters], IV, SC 5 bis, p. 86; MAXIMOS THE CONFESSOR, *Centuries sur la charité* [Centuries on Charity], III, 25, éd. Ceresa-Gastaldo, p. 154; *Questions et difficultés* [Questions and difficulties] III/1,CCSG 10, p. 170; JOHN OF DAMASCUS, *Exposé précis de la foi orthodoxe* [An Exact Exposition of the Orthodox Faith], 26 (II, 12), SC 535, p. 300. These virtues start as a pure potential which the person is called freely to cultivate with the help of God's grace.

17 Cf. J. Gaïth, *La Liberté chez Grégoire de Nysse*, Vrin, Paris, 1953, p. 52.

18 Cf. *La Création de l'homme* [The Creation of man], PG 44, 177D-180A, SC 6, p. 151–2.

19 This remark of St Gregory is aimed at the pagan concepts of the Stoics.

20 *Discours* [Discourses], XXXVIII, 11, SC 358, p. 124.

21 See GREGORY OF NYSSA, *La Création de l'homme* [The Creation of man], II, PG 44, 132D; IV, PG 44, 136BC; JOHN CHRYSOSTOM, *Homélies sur la Genèse* [Homilies on Genesis], VIII, 2, PG 53, 71; XIII, 4, PG 53, 109. See also JOHN OF DAMASCUS, *Exposé précis de la foi orthodoxe* [An Exact Exposition of the Orthodox Faith], 24 (II, 10), SC 535, p. 280: "Before the transgression, all things were placed under man's authority, for God set him as master over all that is on the earth and in the waters." In the same vein, St John Chrysostom compares the world with all its wonders to a palace prepared by God to receive the king (cf. *Traité de la componction* [Treatise on compunction], II, 5).

22 *La Création de l'homme* [The Creation of man], II, PG 44, 132d-133B, SC 6, p. 90–1.

23 See, for example, BASIL OF CAESAREA, *Sur l'origine de l'homme* [On the origin of man], I, 9, SC 160, p. 186–90: JOHN CHRYSOSTOM, *Homélies sur la Genèse* [Homilies on Genesis], IX, 4, PG 53, 78–9; X, 5, PG 53, 86; *Sermons sur la Genèse* [Sermons on Genesis], SC 433, p. 210; JOHN OF DAMASCUS, *Exposé précis de la foi orthodoxe* [An Exact Exposition of the Orthodox Faith], 24 (II, 10), SC 535,

p. 281: "Before the transgression, everything was placed under man's power, for God had set him up as master of all which is upon the earth and in the waters."

24 See GREGORY OF NYSSA, *La Création de l'homme* [The Creation of man], IV, PG 44, 136C.

25 See BASIL OF CAESAREA, *Homélies sur l'Hexaéméron* [Homilies on the six days of Creation], VI, SC 26 bis, p. 328; *Sur l'origine de l'homme* [On the origin of man], I, 9, SC 160, p. 191: "Man received the power to command thanks to the superiority of his reason."

26 See GREGORY OF NYSSA, *La Création de l'homme* [The Creation of man], IV, PG 44, 136BC.

27 GREGORY OF NYSSA refers clearly to this in the passage quoted above where he presents man as king of creation (*La Création de l'homme* [The Creation of man], II PG 44, 133A, SC 44, p. 90–1). It has been omitted from the present quotation since it will be used later in our work.

28 These points are further developed below.

29 St Basil also sees here the growth of man through his different stages of life—childhood, youth, maturity, and old age … (*Sur l'origine de l'homme* [On the origin of man], I, 13, SC 160, p. 196–200).

30 Cf. Origène, *Homélies sur la Genèse* [Homilies on Genesis], I, 15, SC 7 bis, p. 68.

31 *A Autolycus* [To Autolycus], II, 24, SC 20, p. 107.

32 Cf. JOHN CHRYSOSTOM, *Homélies sur la Genèse* [Homilies on Genesis], XIV, 2, PG 53, 113.

33 Ibid.

34 Cf. ORIGEN, *Homélies sur la Genèse* [Homilies on Genesis], I, 12, SC 7 bis, p. 54: "… man for whom the whole universe was created … " Origen criticizes Celsus for having a different opinion (*Contre Celse* [Against Celsus], IV, 74, SC 136, p. 366). See also GREGORY OF NYSSA, *La Création de l'homme* [The Creation of man], I, PG 44, 132C, SC 6, p. 89; GREGORY OF NAZINAZE, *Discours* [Discourses], XLIV, PG 36, 612B; JOHN CHRYSOSTOM, *Homélies sur la Genèse* [Homilies on Genesis], VIII, 2, PG 53, 71; XV, 4, PG 53, 123–4; *Sermons sur la Genèse* [Sermons on Genesis], II, SC 433, p. 184: "it was for his sake that the heavens, the earth, the sea and all the rest of the creation were created," 186; JOHN OF DAMASCUS, *Exposé précis de la foi orthodoxe* [An Exact Exposition of the Orthodox Faith], 16 (II, 2), SC 535, p. 224.

35 *Exposé précis de la foi orthodoxe* [An Exact Exposition of the Orthodox Faith], 24 (II, 10), SC 535, p. 278–80.

36 See, amongst others, GREGORY OF NAZIANZE, *Discours* [Discourses], XXVIII, 23–30, SC 250, p. 148–70; JOHN CHRYSOSTOM, *Discours contre ceux qui se scandalisent* [Against those who are scandalized], II, 7; *Homélies sur Anne* [Homilies on Anne], I, 2; MAXIMOS THE CONFESSOR, *Centuries sur la charité* [Centuries on charity], I, 96, éd. Ceresa-Gastaldo, p. 86.

37 *Les Frères Karamazov* [The brothers Karamazov], "La Pléiade," Gallimard, Paris, 1972, p. 316–17.

38 *Prologue d'Ohrid* [Prologue from Ochrid], Homélie, 28 mars, L'Âge d'Homme, Lausanne, 2009, p. 349.

39 An example of this is the teaching of St Silouan the Athonite: "He would say that all things were created to serve man, and so, when necessary, everything could be made use of, but at the same time, man was obliged to care for all creation. Therefore harm done unnecessarily to an animal—to plant life even—gainsays the law of grace" (ARCHIMANDRITE SOPHRONY, *Starets Silouan, moine du Mont Athos*, Editions Présence; Sisteron 1973, p. 92). [Starets Silouane, Monk of Mount Athos Essex 1991, p. 96].

40 See ORIGEN, *Homélies sur la Genèse* [Homilies on Genesis], I, 17, SC 7 bis, p. 70, and especially BASIL OF CAESAREA, *Sur l'origine de l'homme* [On the origin of man], II, 6, SC 160, p. 238–44; *Homélies*, I, *Sur le jeûne* [Homilies, I, On fasting], 3, PG 31, 168BC et 5, PG 31, 169B. Origen and St Basil make plain that it has only after the flood that God allowed Noah to eat meat as the book of Genesis states: "Every moving thing that liveth shall be meat for you; even as the green herb have I given you all things. But flesh with the life thereof, which is the blood thereof, shall ye not eat" (Gen 9:3–4).

41 *Homélies*, I, *Sur le jeûne* [Homilies, I, On fasting], 3, PG 31, 168B.

42 BASIL OF CAESAREA, *Sur l'origine de l'homme* [On the origin of man], I, 9, SC 160, p. 190.

43 See JOHN CASSIAN, *Conférences* [Conferences], VIII, 21, SC 54, p. 29–30.

44 According to JOHN CASSIAN the descendants of Cain lost "the knowledge and wisdom" of the first man, "which could see the properties of all things." This knowledge degenerated into "occult knowledge" and spiritual power into magic (ibid., p. 30–1).

45 *Sur le paradis* [On Paradise], XI, 51.

46 ORIGEN, *Homélies sur la Genèse* [Homilies on Genesis], I, 16, SC 7 bis, p. 68; BASIL OF CAESAREA, *Sur l'origine de l'homme* [On the origin of man], I, 8, SC 160, p. 182–6; 19, p. 216–18.

47 The Divine Liturgy of Our Father among the Saints John Chrysostom (Jordanville: Hoy Trinity Monastery, 2015), p. 175.

48 Cf. JOHN CHRYSOSTOM, *Homélies sur la Genèse* [Homilies on Genesis], VIII, 2, PG 53, 71; XV, 4, PG 53, 123–4.

49 Cf. THEOPHILOS OF ANTIOCH, *À Autolycus* [To Autolycus], II, 24, SC 20, p. 107.

50 See, for instance, CLEMENT OF ALEXANDRIA, *Stromates*, VII, 35, 1–7, SC 428, p. 126–8; GREGORY OF NAZINZE, *Discours* [Discourses], XXVIII, 23–30, SC 250, p. 148–70; THEODORET OF CYR, *Discours sur la Providence* [Discourses on Providence], V, PG 83, 624D-641C.

51 *Discours catéchétique* [Catechetical discourses], 25, SC 453, p. 258.

52 *Lettres spirituelles* [Spiritual letters], n° 78, L'Âge d'Homme, Lausanne, 2005, p. 223.

53 *Centuries sur la charité* [Centuries on charity], I, 96.

54 *Cent cinquante chapitres* 78, *Philocalie des Pères neptiques* [One hundred and fifty chapters 78, Philokalia], vol. 10, Abbaye de Bellefontaine, Bégrolles-en-Mauges, 1990, p. 264.

55 The world may be considered as being in God, but only in the form of the ideas of His Will, which St Maximos calls the *logoi* (see the next section).

56 This confusion is found frequently in the work of M.M. EGGER quoted above *La Terre comme soi-même*, despite the author's claim to represent the Orthodox Tradition.

57 *Cent cinquante chapitres*, 78, *Philocalie des Pères neptiques* [One hundred and fifty chapters 78, Philokalia], vol. 10, Abbaye de Bellefontaine, Bégrolles-en-Mauges, 1990, p. 264.

58 See the next section.

59 For a description of the thought of the Greek Fathers on the Divine energies, see my work *La Théologie des énergies divines. Des origines à saint Jean Damascène*, Éditions du Cerf, Paris, 2010.

60 *Homélies* [Homilies], 34, Pour la Transfiguration, PG 151, 424B, in GREGORY PALAMAS, *Homélies* [Homilies], YMCA-PRESS/O.E.I.L, Paris, 1987, p. 185.

61 *Homélies sur 2 Corinthiens* [Homilies on 2 Corinthians], XV, 2.

62 *Centuries sur la théologie et l'économie du Fils de Dieu* [Centuries on the theology and the economy of the Son of God], I, 10.

63 *Contre les hérésies* [Against the heresies], IV, 19, 2, SC 100, p. 618–20.

64 *À Autolycus* [To Autolycus], I, 5–7, trad. M. de Genoude.

65 *Discours* [Discourses], XXVIII, 23–30, SC 250, p. 148–70.

66 *Discours sur la Providence* [Discourses on Providence], V, PG 83, 624D-641C.

67 *Homélie pour la Théophanie,* dans *Homélies pour les dimanches et les jours de fêtes* [Homily for the Theophany, in Homilies for Sundays and Feast Days], L'Âge d'Homme, Lausanne, 2016, p. 98–9.

68 The *logoi* are sometimes assimilated to the divine energies. In reality, they are distinct from them as I have shown in my work "La conception maximinienne des energies divine et des *logoi* et la théorie platonicienne des Idées," *ΦΙΛΟΘΕΟΣ. International Journal of Philosophy and Theology,* 4, 2004, p. 276–83. There is a more developed presentation of this most important concept of St Maximos in my book: *La Divinisation de l'homme selon saint Maxime le Confesseur,* Éditions du Cerf, Paris, 1996, p. 112–23.

69 Cf. *Questions à Thalassios* [Questions to Thalassios], 64, PG 90, 709B, CCSG 22, p. 211.410.

70 Cf. ibid., 65, PG 90, 744D, CCSG 22, p. 263.204–5.

71 Cf. *Ambigua à Jean,* 7 [Ambigua to John, 7], PG 91, 1077C; *Lettres,* 12, PG 91, 485D.

72 Cf. *Lettres* [Letters], 12, PG 91, 485D.

73 Cf. *Ambigua à Jean,* 7 [Ambigua to John, 7], PG 91, 1080A; 21, PG 91, 1245B.

74 Cf. ibid., 41, PG 91, 1309C. *Thal.,* 2, PG 90, 272AB, CCSG 7, p. 51.12–19.

75 Cf. *Questions à Thalassios* [Questions to Thalassios], 2, PG 90, 272A, CCSG 7, p. 51.7–9.

76 Cf. *Ambigua à Jean,* 7 [Ambigua to John, 7], PG 91, 1081A; 42, PG 91, 1328A.

77 Cf. ibid., PG 91, 1081A. *Thal.,* 13, PG 90, 293D-296A, CCSG 7, p. 51.6–7.

78 Cf. *Ambigua à Jean,* 42 [Ambigua to John, 42], PG 91, 13281B, 1329BC.

79 Cf. ibid., 7, PG 91, 1081A; 42, PG 91, 1328AB. *Thal.,* 60, PG 90, 625A, CCSG 22, p. 81.130.

80 Cf. *Ambigua à Jean,* 7 [Ambigua to John, 7], PG 91, 1081A; 42, PG 91, 1328B.

81 Cf. *Questions à Thalassios* [Questions to Thalassios], 2, PG 90, 272A, CCSG 7, p. 51.7–12.

82 Cf. ibid., 60, PG 90, 625A, CCSG 22, p. 81.126–30.

83 Cf. *Amb. Io.,* 7 [Ambigua to John, 7], PG 91, 1080A.

84 Cf. ibid., PG 91, 1085A. *Thal.* [Questions to Thalassios], 13, PG 90, 296A, CCSG 7, p. 95.8. PSEUDO DIONYSIOS *Sur les noms divins* [On the divine names], V, 8, PG 3, 824C.

85 Cf. *Questions à Thalassios* [Questions to Thalassios], 13, PG 90, 296A, CCSG 7, p. 95.9–13.

86 *Ambigua à Jean,* 7 [Ambigua to John, 7], PG 91, 1077C-1080B.

87 *Questions à Thalassios* [Questions to Thalassios], 51, SC 554, p. 142–4.
88 Ibid., p. 144.
89 *Homélies sur l'Hexaéméron* [Homilies on the six days of Creation], V, 9, SC 26 bis, p. 318.
90 Ibid., 3, SC 26 bis, p. 290.
91 The Festal Menaion, trans Mother Mary and Archimandrite Kallistos Ware (London: Faber and Faber, 1984), p. 356.
92 *Lettres spirituelles* [Spiritual Letters], n° 62, L'Âge d'Homme, Lausanne, 2005, p. 197.
93 *À Autolycus* [To Autolycus], II, 16, 17, SC 20, p. 98–100.
94 *Homélies sur l'Hexaéméron* [Homilies on the six days of Creation], SC 26 bis, Cerf, Paris, 1968.
95 See *Discours* [Discourses], XXVIII, 23–30, SC 250, p. 148–70.
96 See, for instance, *Homélies sur les statues, au peuple d'Antioche* [Homilies on statues to the people of Antioch], XII, 2–3; *Homélies sur Anne* [Homilies on Anne], I, 2; *Discours contre ceux qui se scandalisent* [Against those who are scandalized], II, 7; *Homélies sur les Actes*[Homilies on Acts], XXXIV, 5; *Homélies sur 1 Thessaloniciens* [Homilies on 1 Thessalonians], X, 2–3.
97 *Discours sur la Providence* [Discourses on Providence], PG 83, 556B-773B, trad. Les Belles Lettres, Paris, 1954.
98 EVAGRIUS PONTICUS, *Traité pratique* [Practical treatise], 92, SC 171, p. 694.
99 *Mystagogie* [Mystagogy], 2, PG 90, 669A-D.
100 Quoted by Patriarch Bartholomew. A Message for the day of prayer for the Creation, September 1, 1993.
101 See *La Création de l'homme* [The Creation of man], II, PG 44, 133A.
102 See *Exposé précis de la foi orthodoxe* [An Exact Exposition of the Orthodox Faith], 25 (II, 11), SC 535, p. 288 et 290; 44 (II, 30), p. 368.
103 *Lettres spirituelles* [Spiritual Letters], n° 62, L'Âge d'Homme, Lausanne, 2005, p. 197.
104 Quoted in *Saints Peter and Paul Orthodox Church,* Newsletter, Avril 2005, p. 2–3.
105 *Questions à Thalassios* [Questions to Thalassios], Introduction, CCSG 7, p. 37.331–2.
106 Ibid., p. 37.332–4.
107 Cf. *Questions à Thalassios* [Questions to Thalassios] 51, CCSG 7, p. 395; *Ambigua à Jean*, 10 [Ambigua to John, 10], PG 91, 1137AC; 60, PG 91, 1385AB.

108 See my work *Thérapeutique des maladies spirituelles,* 6e éd., Cerf, Paris, 2013, p. 767–76.

109 The phrase used by Hans Urs von Balthazar in his study of St Maximos.

110 At his baptism, man is given a liturgical function as "king, priest and prophet." In our day there are those who theorize about "the universal priesthood of the laity," understanding it in a liturgical and clerical fashion and treating laymen as co-liturgists equal to the ordained ministers. These ideas I have criticized elsewhere. It can easily be shown that the Fathers saw in this formula an expression of the new and exceptional state conferred on a Christian at baptism. They saw his liturgical function as an offering, first of himself to God, and then of all other creatures in his life. (See *La Vie sacramentelle,* Éditions du Cerf, Paris, 2014, p. 40–1.)

111 Cf. *Questions à Thalassios* [Questions to Thalassios], Introduction, CCSG 7, p. 37.340–9.

112 *Contre les hérésies* [Against the Heresies], IV, 18, 6, SC 100, p. 612.

113 *La Création de l'homme* [The Creation of man], PG 44, 132D-133A, SC 6, p. 90–1. The beginning of this text and what follows have been quoted above.

114 Cf. JOHN CHRYSOSTOM, *Homélies sur la Genèse* [Homilies on Genesis], XIV, 5, PG 53, 116; XV, 4, PG 53, 124; *Sermons sur la Genèse* [Sermons on Genesis], III, 2, SC 433, p. 210.

115 See *Ambigua à Jean,* 7 [Ambigua to John, 7], PG 91, 1092BC et surtout 41, PG 91, 1305B-1308C.

116 These poles were as follows: (1) created nature as against uncreated nature (creation as against God); (2) within created nature, perceptible beings as against intelligible beings; (3) within perceptible creation, the earth as against the heavens; (4) on earth, paradise as against the inhabited world; (5) within humanity, man as against woman. This is set forth in *Ambigua à Jean,* 41 [Ambigua to John, 41], PG 91, 1305A-1308C, where St Maximos describes in detail man's task of mediation.

117 See *Questions à Thalassios* [Questions to Thalassios], 51, CCSG 7, p. 395–7, 405; *Ambigua à Jean,* 10 [Ambigua to John, 10], PG 91, 1193CD; 30, PG 91, 1273BC; 41, PG 91, 1305A-1308C.

118 *Ambigua à Jean,* 41 [Ambigua to John, 41], PG 91, 1305BC.

119 See ibid., 7, PG 91, 1092BC.

120 *Discours apologétique* [Apologetic discourse], III, PG 93, 1604AB.

121 This tendency is described, especially, in the book cited above of M.M. EGGER, *La Terre comme soi-même.*

THE SIN OF MANKIND AND ITS ECOLOGICAL CONSEQUENCES

1 See *Questions à Thalassios* [Questions to Thalassios], Prologue, SC 529, p. 134–6.
2 See *Questions à Thalassios* [Questions to Thalassios], Prologue, SC 529, p. 134 et 142.
3 See ibid., p. 134–6.
4 See MAXIMOS THE CONFESSOR, *Questions à Thalassios* [Questions to Thalassios], Prologue, SC 529, p. 140.
5 See *Questions à Thalassios* [Questions to Thalassios], Prologue, SC 529, p. 140.
6 See ibid., p. 136–8.
7 See ibid., p. 142. This idea can be found in GREGORY OF NYSSA, *La Création de l'homme* [The Creation of man], XIX, PG 44, 197 B; XX, PG 44, 197 CD, 200 B; *Discours catéchétique* [Catechetical discourses], VIII, *SC* 453, p. 198, l. 137–9. The idea was also taken up by Freud which he used to justify the necessity for society to impose laws and ethics which constrain people's behavior (*Le Malaise dans la culture*, 1930); but it is nonetheless possible, as in our own day, for society to develop hedonistic ethics which justify the natural habits of fallen nature, rather than trying to set them right.
8 See *Questions à Thalassios* [Questions to Thalassios], Prologue, SC 529, p. 142. This idea is also to be found in GREGORY OF NYSSA, *La Création de l'homme* [The Creation of man], XIX, PG 44, 197 B; XX, PG 44, 197 CD, 200 B; *Discours catéchétique* [Catechetical discourses], VIII, *SC* 453, p. 198, l. 137–9.
9 See JOHN CHRYSOSTOM, *Homélies sur la Genèse* [Homilies on Genesis], XVII, 9, PG 53, 116.
10 See ibid.
11 See ISAAC THE SYRIAN, *Discours ascétiques* [Ascetical Homilies], 62. The classical definition of science is: "The knowledge of phenomena and their laws." Phenomena are, etymologically (from the verb *phareinl to appear*), those things which appear to the naked senses, or to the senses through instruments.
12 See ibid.
13 See JOHN CASSIAN, *Conférences* [Conferences], VIII, 21.
14 Even in fairly recent times the link between science and the occult remained. For example, chemistry was closely linked with alchemy right up to the beginning of the eighteenth century.
15 CLEMENT OF ALEXANDRIA, *Stromates*, II, iv, 13, 3.
16 *Ambigua à Jean* [Ambigua to John], 45, PG 91, 1353C-1356B.

17 *Triades pour la défense des saints hésychastes* [Triads in defense of the holy hesychasts], I, 1, 7, éd. Meyendorff, Louvain, 1973, p. 23.

18 *Discours ascétiques* [Ascetical Homlies], LXII-LXV, 11 [alias LXIII], trad. du P. Placide Deseille, Saint Laurent-en-Royans et Solan, 2006, p. 401.

19 Translators note. The text in italics is from *The ascetical homilies of St Isaac the Syrian*, 52, p. 259 (Brookline, MA: The Holy Transfiguration Monastery 1984). Note that the English translation numbers the homilies differently to the French translation, which follows the Greek printed text. A key to the correspondence is on p. cxiii-cxv of the English translation.

20 See my works on sicknesses: *Thérapeutique des maladies spirituelles*, 6e éd., Paris, 2013; *Thérapeutique des maladies mentales*, 2e éd., Paris, 2007; *Théologie de la maladie* [On the sicknesses of the body], 3e éd., Paris, 2001.

21 See *La création de l'homme* [The Creation of man], XII, PG 44 161C-164B, SC 6, p. 131–3.

22 See my work *Maxime le Confesseur, médiateur entre l'Orient et l'Occident*, Cerf, Paris, 1998, ch. 2, "The question of Adam's legacy," I, "The way original sin is transmitted," p. 80–2.

23 *Homélies spirituelles*, [Spiritual Homilies] (coll. II), XI, 5, Abbaye de Bellefontaine, Bégrolles en Mauges, 1984, p. 159.

24 *Lettres* [Letters], X, PG 91, 449B.

25 *Sur l'incarnation du Verbe* [On the Incarnation of the Word], XLIII, 3, SC 199, p. 420.

26 The Fathers follow popular wisdom in using certain animals as models of virtue or vice. The relationship of predator with prey is often extremely cruel. Yet though the violence of animals may remain within the limits needed for their survival, they retain their violent character of objective evil. In contrast, man's violence may be gratuitous or a source of pleasure.

27 They fall ill or decline, are corrupted, wither, decay, rot, and die.

28 For example, DOSTOEVSKI writes: "The bear is terrible and ferocious but is not responsible for this" (*Les Carnets des Frères Karamazov* [The Brothers Karamazov], "La Pléiade," Gallimard, Paris, 1972, p. 887). See also Apophtegmes, série alphabétique (Sayings of the Desert Fathers, alphabetical series), Poemen 41. "The animals without reason are not reprehensible."

29 *Septième ton, Vêpres du lundi* [Monday vespers in the 7th tone], Lucernaire, in *Paraclitique ou Grand Octoèque*, trad. du P. Denis Guillaume, 2e éd., Parme, 1995, p. 579 [italics added].

30 V. LOSSKY, *Théologie dogmatique* [Dogmatic Theology], Paris, 2012, p. 116.

31 *Homélies sur les statues* [Homilies on the statues], IX, 4.
32 *Traités éthiques* [Ethical treatises], I, 2, SC 122, p. 190.
33 See *Pensées,* éd. Brunschvicg, n° 139.
34 See *Leviathan,* London 1651.
35 See *Le malaise dans la culture,* Londres, 1948; trad. française Paris, 1995.
36 See *Discours sur l'origine et les fondements de l'inégalité parmi les hommes,* Amsterdam, 1755.
37 See, for instance, BERNADIN DE SAINT PIERRE, *Études sur la nature,* Paris, 1784; *Paul et Virginie,* Paris, 1788; *Harmonies de la nature,* Paris, 1815.
38 Prayer Book, Fourth Edition—Revised (Jordanville, New York: Holy Trinity Publications, 2005), p. 8.
39 On this subject, see my paper "The Mode of Deification," in P. ALLEN and B. NEIL (éd.), *The Oxford Handbook of Maximus the Confessor,* Oxford: Oxford University Press, 2015, p. 340–59.
40 On the difference between these two approaches, see the classic work of J.S. ROMANIDES, *The Ancestral Sin: A Comparative Study of the Sin of Our Ancestors Adam and Eve According to the Paradigms and Doctrines of the First and Second Century Church and the Augustinian Formulation of Original Sin,* Glen Rock, 2002.
41 See ST JOHN CHRYSOSTOM, *Sermons sur la Genèse* [Sermons on Genesis], V, SC 433, p. 252.
42 See ST JOHN CHRYSOSTOM, *Sermons sur la Genèse* [Sermons on Genesis], V, SC 433, p. 252.

HOW DID WE REACH THE PRESENT SITUATION?

1 See *Pensées,* éd. Brunschvicg, n° 282.
2 *Le Nouvel esprit scientifique,* Alcan, 1934.
3 The writings of the native tribes of North America are extremely touching in this regard. They witness to a refined vision of nature in contrast with the brutality of the whites. See particularly J.E. BROWN, *L'Héritage spirituel des Indiens d'Amérique* [The spiritual Legacy of the American Indians], Paris, 1990; T.C. McCLUHAN, *Pieds nus sur la terre sacrée,* Paris, 1995.
4 One of the main architects of this Christian anthropology which rejects dualism was St Irenaeos of Lyon. See my book *Théologie du corps,* Paris, 2009, p. 13–21.
5 *Discours de la méthode,* 4th part: "Then, attentively examining what I was, I saw that I could pretend to have no body, that the world did not exist, nor any place where I might be; but despite this, I could in no way pretend that I was not. Quite

the contrary, the very fact that I could think of doubting the truth of other things showed most clearly and surely that I was. Whereas had I simply ceased to think, even though everything else that I had imagined were true, I would have had no reason to believe that I was. From this I knew that I was a substance of which the whole essence or nature is simply to think, and to be had no need of place or any material thing. So this I, that is to say the soul by which I am what I am, is entirely distinct from the body, and it is easier to know it than to know the body; and were this body not to exist, the soul would not cease to be all that it is."

6 Ibid.

7 Ibid.

8 PASCAL himself said of Descartes: "I cannot forgive Descartes. In all his philosophy he would have been delighted to get rid of God, but he was unable to avoid giving Him the trivial task of setting the world in motion. Apart from that, he had no need of God." (*Pensées*), éd. Brunschvicg, n° 77.

9 *Encyclopédie* (1765), article "Naturalistes."

10 *Encyclopédie* (1765), article "Encyclopédie."

11 *Addition aux Pensées philosophiques.*

12 Diderot writes, for example: "You mix theology into philosophy. You spoil everything by mixing lies into truth. Theology should be cut down" (*Reproche fait à des Anglais* [1781]).

13 For Rousseau, the conscience itself is an instinct, "divine" perhaps, but not in a way which could bring man to "the likeness of God" (*L'Émile* [1762]).

14 We can recall this emblematic tale, taken from the treasury of ancient Chinese wisdom: "Tzeu-Koung, a disciple of Confucius, after going to the principality of Tch'ou returned again to Tsinn. Close to the river Han, he saw a man who was watering his vegetable garden. He had dug an irrigation ditch. The old man went down to the bottom of the well and filled a bucket with water. Then he carried it in his arms up to the surface and poured it into the ditch. It was hard work for little result. Tzeu-Koung said to him: 'There is a way in which you could fill a hundred ditches in a single day without tiring yourself. Would you not like to learn it?' At these words, the gardener stood up and looked at him saying: 'What is this way?' Tzeu-Koung replied: 'You take a rod of wood, weighted at one end and light at the other. In this way you can draw water so fast that it might be a spring.' At this, the face of the old man became dark with anger, and he said: 'I learnt from my master that he who uses a machine does his work mechanically. He who works mechanically ends up with the heart of a machine, and he who bears in his breast the heart of a machine loses his native wit. He who loses his

native wit becomes troubled in his soul, and the trouble in his soul prevents the Principal from dwelling peacefully in his heart. I am not unaware of the methods of which you speak, but I would be ashamed to use them.' Abashed, Tzeu-Koung hung his head and made no reply" (Tchouang-Tzeu, *Nan-hoa-tchen-king*, Chapitre 12K, in L. WEIGER, *Les Pères du système taoïste*, Éditions Les Belles Lettres, Paris, 1950, p. 300–301 [modified translation]).

15 See *Politics*, I.

16 See *Die protestantische Ethik und der "Geist" des Kapitalismus*, in *Archiv für Sozialwissenschaft und Sozialpolitik*, 1904–1905; trad. fr. *L'Éthique protestante et l'esprit du capitalisme*, Paris, 2004.

17 See F. BRAUDEL, *La Dynamique du capitalisme*, Arthaud, 1985.

18 In the seventeenth century this knowledge was unified, philosophy being seen at that time as including all the sciences. We see this, for example, in the *Discours de la méthode* of Descartes.

19 One of its main representatives, Auguste Comte reveals himself to be at once atheist ("In the end, God is no more needed to love or to weep than to judge or to think" [*Letter to Mme Austin*, avril 4, 1844]) and therefore humanist ("In the end, nothing is real but humanity") and relativist ("All is relative, and that is the only absolute").

20 C. LEVI-STRAUSS remarks that "Their ideal is to continue to live as their ancestors always lived, following all their customs, and to believe exactly what their ancestors have always believed" (*Conférence à l'ORTF* du, January 21, 1968). The traditional mind, so called to contrast it with the modern mind, has been well analyzed in the works of Mircea Eliade, the historian of religions.

21 *Du progrès et de l'accroissement des* sciences [The Advancement and Proficience of Learning Divine and Human] (1605).

22 *Cours de philosophie positive* (1830–1842).

23 *Catéchisme positiviste* (1852).

24 *La Nouvelle Atlantide* [The New Atlantis], Garnier-Flammarion, Paris, 1997, p. 119.

25 *Considération sur la marche des idées et des événements dans les temps modernes*, Paris, 1872, V, 6.

26 Original edition *Die protestantische Ethik und der Geist des Kapitalismus* (1904–1905).

27 "Sensual pleasure" is here opposed to "spiritual joy" and is not simply confined to the body, its sexuality or its food.

28 Christmas message, 2008.

29 *Commentaire sur Isaïe* [Commentary on Isaiah], V, 4–5.

30 On the perversion and alienation of desire in fallen man, see my work *Thérapeutique des maladies spirituelles*, 6e éd., Paris, 2013, p. 75–86.

31 Amongst the Fathers it is St Gregory of Nyssa who goes most deeply into this subject which has been given the name of "epectasis." See especially his *Vie de Moïse* [Life of Moses], II, 219–48, p. 256–76.

RESTORING THE RELATIONSHIP OF MAN WITH NATURE

1 It is, to say the least paradoxical and inconsistent in the first two cases to see those who advocate a policy of murdering human persons at the beginning and the end of their lives to be so concerned about the "rights of animals"; and in the last three cases to see the promotion of unnatural practices which run counter to the survival of the human race.

2 A summary of his speeches and publications can be found in JOHN CHRYSSAVGIS, "Le patriarche oecuménique Bartholomée: aperçus sur une vision du monde chrétien orthodoxe," *Revue internationale des études de l'environnement*, 64, 2007, p. 9–18. Amongst his contributions we may single out: "La dimension eucharistique, ascétique et spirituelle du sacrifice," Discours de clôture du Symposium "Religion, science et environnement," Venise, juin 10, 2002; "Religion et environnement, quels défis spirituels pour aujourd'hui ?," Discours à l'Institut catholique de Paris le, janvier 30, 2014; *Et Dieu vit que cela était bon*, Cerf, Paris, 2015.

3 *Lettre encyclique sur l'environnement*, septembre 1, 1989.

4 *Les bases de la conception sociale de l'Église orthodoxe russe*, chapitre XIII, Moscou, 2000; trad. fr., Éditions du Cerf, Paris, 2007.

5 *La position de l'Église orthodoxe russe sur les questions environnementales importantes* (2013).

6 See especially T.DELAHAYE, *Le Monastère de Solan. Une aventure agroécologique*, Actes Sud, Arles, 2011.

7 See Cf. ORIGEN, *Homélies sur Jérémie* [Homilies on Jeremiah], XIV, 1–2, SC 238, p. 64–8. ANTHONY THE GREAT, *Lettres* [Letters], II, 2; III, 2; IV, 2; V, 2, in SAINT ANTHONY, *Lettres* [Letters], "Spiritualité orientale," n° 19, Bégrolles-en-Mauges, 1976, p. 52–3, 59–60, 64–5, 86–7. GREGORY OF NAZIANZE, *Discours* [Discourses], XLV, 9, PG 36, 643BC; XXXVIII, 13, SC 358, p. 130–2; GREGORY OF NYSSA, *Vie de Moïse* [The life of Moses], II, 261, SC 1, p. 284–6;

272, SC 1, p. 290; 278, SC 1, p. 294; MACARIOS OF EGYPT, *Homélies* [Homilies], (Coll. II), XX, 4–6, PTS 4, p. 189–90; *Homélies* [Homilies], (Coll. III), XXIV, 3–4, SC 275, p. 264–6; CYRIL OF JERUSALEM, *Catéchèses baptismales* [Baptismal Catechisms], XII, 6–8, PG 33, 732B-736A; DOROTHEOS OF GAZA *Instructions spirituelles* [Spiritual Instructions], I, 3–4, SC 92, p. 150–2.

8 Cf. JOHN CLIMACOS, *L'Échelle* [The Ladder], I, 19.

9 The Divine Liturgy of Our Father among the Saints John Chrysostom, p. 171.

10 The Divine Liturgy of Our Father among the Saints John Chrysostom, p. 163.

11 *Contre les hérésies* [Against the Heresies], V, 18, 3, SC 153, p. 244–6. A little further on St Irenaeus repeats that "the Lord came manifestly into his own domain" and "was borne up by His own creation which He Himself sustains" (ibid., 19, 1, p. 248).

12 *Vie et paroles*, L'Âge d'Homme, Lausanne, p. 122–3.

13 This is the opinion of M.M. EGGER, M. M. Egger, *La Terre comme soi-même*, Genève, 2012, p. 141, et 143. There, he writes that "God made himself the flesh of the Cosmos so that the Cosmos might be divinized." He also sees Christ as "the soul of the world" (p. 146) an idea which comes from pagan cosmologies.

14 As in the work of Matthew Fox, *Le Christ cosmique*, Albin Michel, Paris, 1995.

15 See *Ambigua à Jean* [Ambigua to John], 33, PG 91, 1285C-1288A.

16 Cf. ibid., 1308CD.

17 Ibid., 7, PG 91, 1092C.

18 Especially *Thérapeutique des maladies spirituelles*, 6e éd., Cerf, Paris, 2013.

19 *Théologie de la maladie*, 3e éd., Cerf, Paris, 2001, p. 40–4.

20 Cf. ST JOHN OF DAMASCUS, *Exposé précis de la foi orthodoxe* [An Exact Exposition of the Orthodox Faith], 92 (IV, 19), SC 540, p. 266. ST IRENAEOS OF LYON *Contre les hérésies* [Against the Heresies], IV, 37, SC 100, p. 918–42.

21 For example, volcanic eruptions pollute the air and remove ozone from the atmosphere; and certain minerals, along with the corpses of animals or rotting plants pollute the water.

22 The Divine Liturgy of Our Father among the Saints John Chrysostom, p. 75.

23 *Paix et joie dans le Saint-Esprit*, L'Âge d'Homme, Lausanne, 2010, p. 126.

24 For more details, see my work *Thérapeutique des maladies spirituelles*, 6e éd., Cerf, Paris, 2013, p. 596–8.

25 For more details, see my work *Thérapeutique des maladies spirituelles*, 6e éd., Cerf, Paris, 2013, p. 563–72.

26 "La dimension eucharistique, ascétique et spirituelle du sacrifice," Discours de clôture du Symposium "Religion, science et environnement," Venise, juin 10, 2002.

27 Ibid.

28 For further details, see my work *La Vie liturgique*, Cerf, Paris, 2016, p. 111–51.
29 See ORIGEN, *Homélies sur la Genèse* [Homilies on Genesis], I, 17, SC 7 bis, p. 70. BASIL OF CAESAREA, *Sur l'origine de l'homme* [On the origin of man], II, 6, SC 160, p. 238–44; *Homélies, I, Sur le jeûne* [Homilies, I, on fasting], 3, PG 31, 168BC; 5, PG 31, 169B.
30 *Homélies sur Matthieu* [Homilies on Matthew], LXXVII, 6, PG 58, 710.
31 *Homélies sur les statues* [Homilies on the statues], III, 4, PG 49, 53.
32 *Homélies* [Homilies], XIII, 9, PG 151, 161.
33 This is what Christ meant when he commanded us to love our neighbor *as ourself.* It means being in our spiritual reality as God envisages us.
34 *Variations sur la charité*, Cerf, Paris, 2007.
35 *Les Frères Karamazov*, "La Pléiade," Gallimard, Paris, 1972, p. 343.
36 Morality cannot be absolute without the Absolute—God—as its foundation. Dostoievski summed this up in his famous epithet: "If God does not exist, then everything is allowed."
37 "La Pyramide paradisiaque," dans *La foi et la vie selon l'Évangile*, L'Âge d'Homme, Lausanne, 2007, p. 148.
38 Do you know that God has given us another commandment which is not written in Scripture? It is the commandment: "Love the trees." "When you plant a tree, you plant hope, you plant peace, you plant love and you will receive the blessing of God." Quoted by P. NIKITARAS, *O Gerontas Amphilochios Makris: Mia synchroni morphi tis Patmou*, Athènes, 1984, p. 47–9 and I.L. TRIANTIS, *O Gerontas tis Patmou Amphilochios Makris*, Patmos, 1997, p. 139.
39 *Discours ascétiques*, LXXXI, 2, Saint Laurent-en-Royans et Solan, 2006, p. 469–70. [Ascetical Homilies, 71, Brookline 1984 p. 344–5].
40 *Paix et joie dans le Saint-Esprit*, L'Âge d'Homme, Lausanne, 2010, p. 199.
41 ARCHIMANDRITE SOPHRONY, *Starets Silouane, moine de Mont-Athos. Vie-Doctrine-Écrits*, Éditions Présence, Sisteron, 1973, p. 423. [Starets Silouan, Essex 1991, p. 469].
42 *Théologie dogmatique orthodoxe*, t. I.
43 *Vie et paroles*, L'Âge d'Homme, Lausanne, p. 281.
44 *Vie et paroles*, L'Âge d'Homme, Lausanne, p. 279.
45 *Anthologie des conseils*, L'Âge d'Homme, Lausanne, p. 32.
46 *Protreptique* [Protrepticus], X, 94, 2–3, SC 2, p. 162.
47 *Stromates*, VII, 35, 1–7, SC 428, p. 126–8.
48 This is the name given to those Church Fathers who in the very first centuries defended Christianity against anti-Christian religions, philosophies, and politics.

49 Preface to M. M. EGGER, in his work *La Terre comme soi-même*, Genève, 2012, p. IV.
50 Letter of November 26, 1976, to the sisters of the monastery of Souroti in *Lettres*, Souroti, 2005, p. 212–13.
51 *Paix et joie dans le Saint-Esprit*, L'Âge d'Homme, Lausanne, 2010, p. 174.
52 Ibid., p. 214–15.
53 Ibid., p. 318.

Index

HOLY TRINITY PUBLICATIONS
JORDANVILLE, NEW YORK

PRINTSHOP OF SAINT JOB OF POCHAEV

HOLY TRINITY SEMINARY PRESS

The New Media Epidemic

The Undermining of Society, Family, and Our Own Soul

By Jean-Claude Larchet

If we realize how gravely sick is our civilization, we may gain strength to resist. Philosopher and patrologist Dr Jean-Claude Larchet, renowned for his examinations of patristic writings on the causes and consequences of spiritual and physical illness, here tackles the pressing question of the societal and personal effects of our use of new media. His meticulous diagnosis concludes with a discussion of the ways individuals might limit and counteract the deleterious consequences of this new epidemic.

ISBN: 9780884654711

Life after Death According to the Orthodox Tradition

Contemplations on God and the World

By Jean-Claude Larchet
Translated by G. John Champoux

This book offers an accessible and well organized synthesis of the ancient Christian understanding of death and the afterlife. It explains both the time and modalities of the bodily resurrection, the nature of the Particular and the Universal judgments, and of the Church's intercessory prayer for the departed. Larchet notes divergences between eastern and western traditions have existed since the fifth century. A benefit to those who desire to become acquainted with the fullness of the Orthodox Christian tradition on death and the afterlife.

ISBN: 9780884654773